OUR SPECIAL THANKS TO CONTRIBUTORS OF

THE *Taste of Central Asia* COOKBOOK

ON **INDIEGOGO** FUNDRAISING CAMPAIGN.

NICK ROWAN

GULZADA HAMRA

SHAHSANEM MURRAY

TURAN WAHABZADAH

RASHID S

ELMIRA (SA)

PETER OC

PATRICK COMEY

TOM SEYMOUR

GREGOR MOWAT

SUSANNE SPIES-LOESER

RICHARD HEIDER

MARGADANT LAURENT

GULJAMAL PIRENOVA

E AN

NS

Hertfordshire Press © 2016
9 Cherry bank, Chapel Street
Hemel Hempstead, Herts
HP2 5DE, United Kingdom
www.hertfordshirepress.com

THE *Taste of Central Asia* COOKBOOK

Authors: Danny Gordon ©, Elena Bosler-Guseva ©
Editor: Christopher Schwartz, Nick Rowan
Design: Aleksandra Vlasova

We express our gratitude to:

Ian Claytor, Kyrgyz Food, Aigul Alymkulova, Elena Bosler-Guseva, Susanna Fatyan,
Alexandra Tyan, Christopher Shwartz, Eskliev Mukhtar, Guljamal Pirenova,
Kobil Shokirov, Marat Akhmedjanov, Naz Nazar, Sohir Guljon, Taalbyldy Egemberdiev,
Xander Casey & Eskaliev Mukhtar, Kazakh Academy of Tourism and Sport

*British Library Catalogue in Publication Data
A catalogue record for this book is available from the British Library
Library of Congress in Publication Data
A catalogue record for this book has been requested*

ISBN: 978-1-910886-09-0

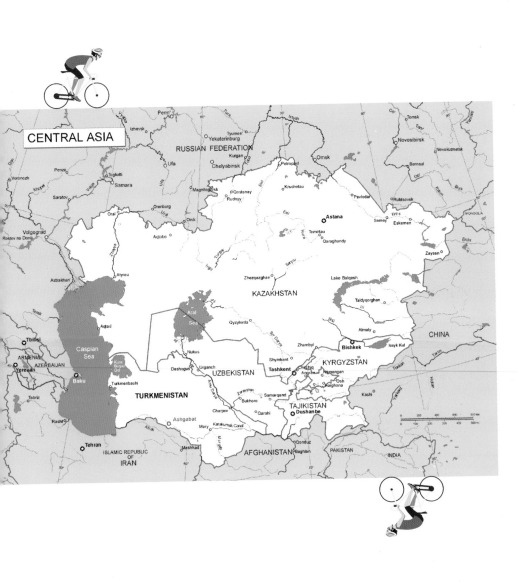

INTRODUCTION

Central Asia may not boast the Michelin starred cuisine of Tokyo, London or Paris, but don't be deceived by those who say it has nothing to offer by way of gastronomic experiences. There are plenty of delights and new foods to try in a cuisine based largely on the region's nomadic heritage that has fused together millennia of itinerant international cuisine. Traditionally this meant horse or sheep's meat, with vegetables hard to come by, but today's Central Asian cuisine has adapted to the modern table, retaining a lingering twist of Soviet and Asian influence that will delight the adventurous and surprise the skeptical.

From the cosmopolitan city of Almaty, Kazakhstan, to the upper limits of the Pamir Highway in Tajikistan, you'll never be far from any of the Central Asian staples of plov, laghman, somsa, manti and shashlyk. Home-cooked food and warm hospitality are the norm extended to any visitor and, as you walk the streets, the smell of something cooking will usually envelope and enrapture all your senses.

A visit to one of the many Central Asian bazaars reveals an array of new and enticing fruits and vegetables that all find their way into Central Asian cuisine. Stall upon stall of frisbee-shaped flatbread, designed to outlast a long desert trek, brings a unique accompaniment to be broken and shared among those you find upon your travels.

4

Slurping tea, the ubiquitous green or black brew offered to guests in delicately decorated crockery, and the cornerstone of the chaikhana (or tea house) culture, join the locals whiling away the hours engaged in deep chatter. However you choose to enjoy the culinary treats Central Asia has to offer, it will undoubtedly be a highlight of your trip and you will yearn for its inimitable flavours on your return.

It is therefore with great pleasure that I introduce you to this edition of The Taste of Central Asia Cookbook. This unique book brings the splendour of the region's cuisine to your home table and will allow you to re-create (and experiment) with your favourite recipes as well as discover new ones. Bring your friends and family and share with them the delights of your connection to Central Asia, whatever it may be. And learn about the places, people and origins of some of Central Asia's most appreciated food along with the striking photography captured in this very special book.

Bon appétit!

Nick Rowan
Editor-in-Chief OCA Magazine

ABOUT AUTHOR

In spring 2012, I cycled through Central Asia, and, as I write, I am living in Bishkek. I have never considered myself a foodie, but during my travels on the bicycle, eating was where the rubber hit the road (pun intended!) with regard to my cultural understanding. This was partly because I was doing it so much, but mostly because it provided my primary source of interaction with the locals and their customs. From being served home-made plov by Kyrgyz policeman in Aktau to eating what I suspected was road-kill shashlik in the Kyzyl-kum desert to brokering new friendships over tea in Dushanbe, I realised the power of food as a way to gain access to this incredible place.

Through lots of trial and error, I began to refine my taste for food in the region and work out where my preferences lay and for which dishes. Every mealtime, I would hear fabulous tales of the origins of local foods, and the superstitions they were shrouded in. This coal-face education has left me fascinated by the sub-text that comes with Central Asian cuisine, and it is my hope that, through this book, I can share some of that sub-text with you.

NOTES FOR THE READER

Central Asia has one of the highest salt-consumption rates in the world, so if you are cautious about your salt-intake, please be aware that the vast majority of meat and dough dishes (as well as many drinks) in the region are prepared with large amounts of salt.

I also want to mention that there are a few dishes that have been included that come with disclaimers about sustainable sourcing. These dishes are part of the cultural heritage and are popular in the regions from which they come. You are likely to encounter them should you visit, which is why I have included them in this book. However, please be aware that in both the Caspian Sea and Issyk-Kul, there is a general threat to biodiversity from overfishing and exploitation. That I have drawn attention to these foods is meant only to inform you of their current status as I have been informed.

Though meat is a large part of Central Asian cuisine, there are foods that are suitable for the vegetarians among you. I have marked these with a $\mathcal{V}$

Lastly, I have included the Cyrillic name for each item so that it is easier to identify on menus. Hopefully this will prevent any confusion when you come to try these delicious tastes.

Welcome !

AKTAU
MANGYSTAU, KAZAKHSTAN

If you could stand on top of Aktau, you might wonder exactly how a place survives in such isolation. Looking west, there is an ocean of water (or more precisely, the largest saltwater lake in the world), and everything that brings, from fish to commerce to oil. Looking east, there is an ocean of sand, camels and infinite roads disappearing into the abyss of the Kyzyl-kum desert.

Founded in 1961 near local uranium fields, the town was formerly called Shevchenko, until its name was changed to Aktau, meaning "white mountain", in 1991. Though Aktau's past may not be the most distinguished, its future should be a different story with the introduction of the "Aktau New City" development project. It seems that plans to establish Aktau as the "pearl of the Caspian" are being taken seriously: parks are being renovated as I write, and I hear constantly of new hotels cropping up.

The fresh fish in Aktau is excellent, and with the influx of chefs as a result of the expansion of the hospitality sector, you should have no problem finding it perfectly prepared.

SAZAN BESHBARMAK

In a twist on the classic Kazakh dish, Beshbarmak, the kind people of Aktau have incorporated fresh fish from the Caspian Sea to create what tastes like an entirely new entity. The dish is usually made with sazan (carp) in aktau, but I have it on good authority that it is also incredibly delicious with salmon.

Ingredients
2kg salmon or carp
500g flour
2 eggs
1 tbsp salt
3-4 onions
1 cup minced chives
3 tbsp minced parsley
3 tbsp oil

Serves: 8 portions

Method
Mix the eggs with the flour and 250ml water to make the dough and add a pinch of salt. Knead the dough until soft and set it aside for 15 minutes. Meanwhile, wash the fish and boil for 15 minutes. Add a pinch of salt.

When ready, take out the fish, remove the skin and bones and carve it into small slices. Roll dough out as flat as possible, and cut it into diamonds (the size is up to you, but not too big). Add the sliced dough to the broth that you used to cook the fish, and boil. Cut the onions into half rings and fry them until transparent.

Dice the parsley. Spread the dough diamonds on a big dish. Cover this base with the fish and fried onions, before sprinkling with parsley to serve.

PISKEN BALYK

Pisken balyk, or boiled fish, is a simple, but beautiful Kazakh dish. The freshness of the fish really makes a difference to the quality of the meal, so try it in Aktau, a stones-throw from the waters from which it was plucked.

Ingredients
1kg carp or catfish
100g carrots, chopped
100g onions, chopped
50ml oil
75g butter
175g tomato purée
750g potatoes
Salt, ground black pepper, cayenne pepper, ground cumin and ground coriander (to taste)

Serves: 4 portions

Method
Fillet the fish and dice the vegetables. Melt the butter in a pan then add the carrots, potatoes and fish. Fry for about 10 minutes, until the vegetables soften.

In the meantime, fry the onion in the oil until golden (about 10 minutes) then stir into the vegetable and fish mix along with the tomato purée. Pour on enough boiling water to cover the mixture, and bring to a simmer.

Season with salt, black pepper and spices. Cook on low heat for about 20 minutes, until all the ingredients are tender. Ladle into deep serving plates and serve with chopped greens.

ALMATY

ALMATY, KAZAKHSTAN

As the largest city in Kazakhstan and the nation's main transport hub, Almaty is the most ethnically and culturally diverse city in the country. Almaty's long-standing significance in the region combined with its international prestige means that it has attracted all manner of cuisine from across Kazakhstan, as well as achieving global gastronomic reach.

I found everything from cheap, local laghman to gourmet French onion soup in Almaty. Coffee houses and quality Chinese, Korean and Italian restaurants mesh seamlessly into Almaty's streetscapes alongside traditional (and not so traditional!) Central Asian eateries.

If you want to get a good feel for Kazakh dining, or grab a slice of home before heading off for an adventure in the nearby mountains, Almaty is a great place to start.

APPLES

With a little digging, you will find that Almaty's old name is Alma-Ata. With a little more, you will find that this means "father of apples". Initially, I thought that this was metaphorical, or a romantic reference to a popular story or myth perhaps. I did not, however, think that the name was meant literally.

A few kilometres away, the slopes of the Tian-Shan Mountains are carpeted with magical wild apple orchards, and the apples that grow there, the "Malus Sieversii", have recently been the subject of some rigorous scientific enquiry. The reason for this interest is because of a long-standing debate about the origins of the domestic apple, "Malus Domestica". Finally, scientists have confirmed that these wild apples do in fact have the genetic profile closest to that of domestic apples.

So, if you love fruit, a trip to Almaty to try a tasty, mythical, "original" apple is a must. If this evokes images of biblical tales, why not try a pomegranate from Turkmenistan...

Interesting fact!
Apples contain no fat,
sodium or cholesterol
and are a good source
of fiber

BAURSAKI

Baursaki is a kind of fried doughnut often served as an appetiser at big meals, or as a snack with tea. Almaty's locals happily tell me of baursaki's significance in making guests feel welcome, and of its place on the dastarkhan (eating place). Don't eat too many at meal-times though; they are exceptionally stodgy, and are almost inevitably followed by giant helpings of plov or beshbarmak.

Ingredients
500g flour
2 tbsp yeast
120ml milk
2 eggs
2 tbsp butter or margarine
1-1.5 tbsp sugar
480ml vegetable oil
A pinch of salt

Method

Mix all the ingredients (except oil) in a large bowl with about 120ml of water to form dough. Take out the dough and knead it on a floured surface, before replacing in the bowl. Cover with a towel and let the mixture sit for 30 minutes.

Heat the oil in deep frying pan using high heat. Make small, disk shaped balls of dough and place carefully into the pan and fry until golden brown. Once cooked, remove excess oil by allowing resting the Baursaki on paper towels. To finish, sprinkle with sugar.

Serves: Roughly 8
(depending on the size of your Baursaki)

BESHBARMAK

This is a dish steeped in cultural importance for the people of Kazakhstan. Though traditionally made with horse meat, you may also see it made with beef or lamb. Beshbarmak literally means "five-fingers" because it is a meal that is eaten, messily in my case, with the hands. All kinds of variations of this can be found easily in Almaty, but if you find yourself becoming a real beshbarmak enthusiast, visit a Kazakh village or two for the truly authentic experience.

Ingredients
2kg lamb on the bone, 500g flour
2 eggs, 1 tbsp salt
3-4 onions, sliced
1 cup minced chives
3 tbsp minced parsley
1 tbsp ground black pepper
1 carrot, diced
3 tbsp oil

Method
Boil the lamb using low heat until the meat flakes easily from the bone (approx. 2.5 hours). As the lamb cooks, mix the flour and eggs with 250ml water, a pinch of salt and some vegetable oil to make the dough for noodles. Flatten and cut into long, thin strips joining the ends to make hoops.

Once the lamb is ready, remove it from the broth, cut the meat into small chunks, and use the broth boil the noodle hoops. Fry chopped onion and carrot together with the lamb until the onion become golden.

Arrange noodles on a big serving plate and top with the lamb. Sprinkle with black pepper and onions. Broth should be served separately in small bowls, sprinkled with diced chives and parsley.

Serves: 8 portions

BASTARTO

For me, bastarto is one of those wonderfully memorable illustrations of Kazakh culinary tradition. The name bastarto refers to the boiled sheep's head that is often served to an honourable guest in a Kazakh home alongside helpings of beshbarmak. While this may seem unusual to those with a Western disposition, it is naturally a tremendous privilege to be served bastarto. Though, this is usually served to men, bastarto will occasionally be given to highly respected women.

Once received, the sheep's head will be carved by the honourable guest who must adhere to a very particular serving ritual. There are subtle variations on this ritual, but during my experience, I was instructed that the tongue was to be served to the youngest girls in order to keep their voices strong; cuts from the nape of the neck to the host; cuts from the cheeks to other guests; and one eyeball each for the honourable guest and the next most highly respected guest (often the oldest man). As the honourable guest, I was also expected to eat the brain. "You can share if you want to", chirped my amiable host in Russian. "But people usually don't!"

Because it is meant as a gift, I cannot guarantee that you will be able to try bastarto. It is of course available to buy it at some restaurants in cities (Almaty being the outstanding example), and even possible to make it at home. However, bastarto is fundamentally used as a sign of respect, and you should count yourself very lucky if you are offered this dish.

Interesting fact!
In rural settings it is a sign of respect to offer the most honoured guest a boiled sheep's head on a beautiful plate.

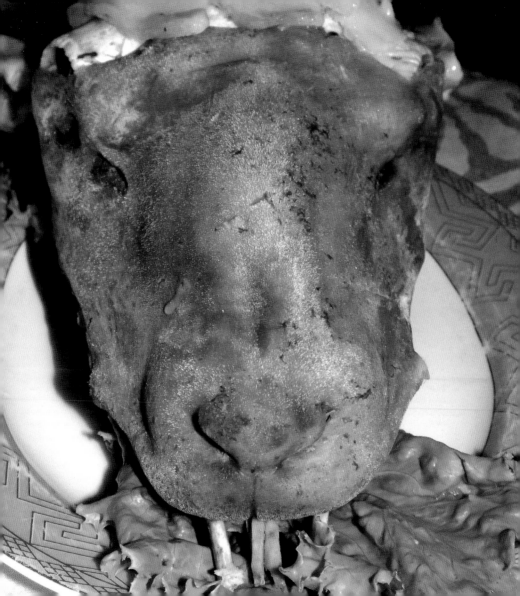

LAGHMAN SHURPA

As the old Kazakh saying goes, "Meat brings strength, shurpa brings beauty". Laghman Shurpa combines both. Initially an import, this Central Asian noodle soup is now incredibly popular in Almaty, and the Kazakhs have made it their own. Variants of this dish can be found on almost every street corner.

Ingredients
700g lamb or beef, cut in strips
vegetable oil
2 peppers (one sweet, one spicy)
2 tomatoes, sliced
1 onion, sliced; 1 carrot, sliced
1 medium turnip, diced; 4 cloves garlic, diced
1l beef broth
30ml white vinegar
salt; 1 batch noodles
basil, cut into strips
red pepper flakes; Sirracha chili sauce

Method
Cut the vegetables into thin strips and dice the turnip and lamb.

Heat a little vegetable oil in a wok or large frying pan using a high heat. When hot, put in the meat and brown it as you stir. Add the vegetables and garlic. Stir-fry for few minutes until everything softens. Add salt and red pepper flakes to taste before adding the beef broth and bringing the mixture to a simmer. Cook until the flavours come together and all the vegetables are tender (approx. 45 min).

Add vinegar and seasoning to taste. Ladle the soup over noodles and garnish with fresh basil, red pepper flakes, and hot sauce.

CHOCOLATE

One of the sweetest surprises you are likely to find in Almaty is the beautiful chocolate produced by the Rakhat Chocolate Company.

Rakhat has been running for over seventy years and is regarded by many locals as the premier chocolate producer in central Asia. According to Rakhat themselves, the organisation began producing confectionary using old equipment rescued from Moscow and Kharkov during the Second World War, making their popularity today even more impressive.

The Rakhat factory in Almaty is well worth a visit. You can go on a tour (though make sure you check opening times), or just salivate over the 300 varieties of confectionary they have in their shop, some of which, it should be noted, are produced especially for diabetics. I tried only a sliver of their selection and have to admit, I have not tasted better chocolate in the region.

Appropriately, "Rakhat" means "pleasure" in Kazakh.

ASHGABAT
ASHGABAT CITY, TURKMENISTAN

Meaning "city of love" in Persian, Ashgabat is sandwiched between the Kopet Dag mountain range and the Kara-Kum desert. Ashgabat is the capital of Turkmenistan, and acts as the nation's glimmering shop window; peering into it will reveal white marble faces of imposing-looking buildings, sitting in sharp relief to golden and blue domes jutting skyward and pastel green parkland. Like Astana, there is clear evidence of the many millions of dollars in natural resource revenues (particularly oil and gas) that have been poured into developing the city.

Since Ashgabat was largely a Russian creation, significant because of its location on the Trans-Caspian railway line, it is unsurprising that there are many elements of Russian cuisine that have been incorporated here. However, as many of the families of Ashgabat sit down around a brightly-coloured cloth laden with pilafs and fresh dairy products, the real surprise is that ancient Turkmen culinary tradition is still so strong. Part of that tradition is a culture of wonderful hospitality, so if one thing is for sure in Ashgabat, it is that you will be warmly received.

DOGRAMA

Dograma (a name taken from the word "dogramak", meaning "to cut to pieces") is considered by many to be the nation's most traditional dish, and is often the food of choice at religious festivals like Gurbalyk (at the end of the Hajj), on the tenth day of Islamic month, Zihijje (Dhu al-Hijjah). While the dograma usually comes soaked in a hot broth, it is also occasionally eaten dry with tea.

Ingredients
1.5kg mutton or beef with fat and bones
3 tbsp salt
2 tomatoes, chopped
1 teaspoon active dry yeast
1 kg flour
2 onions, halved and sliced
Ground black pepper

Serves: 8-10 portions

Method

Put the meat and 5 litres of water in large pot and bring to a boil. Skim off the head of the broth, and add 2 tablespoons of salt. Simmer for 20 minutes (covered), before adding the tomatoes. Continue to simmer until the meat is cooked.

During this process, mix the yeast, flour, 600ml of warm water and 1 tablespoon of salt to make dough. Knead, and make 2 balls of dough. Preheat the oven to 250°C and roll out each ball of dough to a thickness of 1.5cm. Make deep indents in the dough with a fork, brush breads with water and bake until golden brown (15-18 min.).

Tear the bread into small pieces in a large bowl and mix with sliced onion. Place the meat on top, and dice it into the mixture. Mix everything together and drizzle 3-4 tablespoons of broth over the mixture. Cover bowl cloth for 20-30 minutes to let the flavours mingle.

Add black pepper to taste and ladle in enough hot broth to cover the dograma in each serving bowl.

POMEGRANATES

The Kopet Dag mountains, that roll away to the south of Ashgabat, are allegedly both the birthplace of the pomegranate, and the last place on the planet where wild pomegranates grow. Incredibly, this is not the most interesting thing about the fruit.

The pomegranate has incredible cultural and academic significance in Turkmenistan. It is said that the robes of Moses' priests carried the emblem of the pomegranate, and that their image was used to decorate Solomon's temple, as well as having significance in Persian iconography as

a symbol of fertility. Dr G. Levin, a botanist from the Soviet Union, spent almost his entire professional life studying the pomegranate and amassing 1117 varieties of the fruit from around the world in Garrygala, an agricultural research station just north of the Iran border.

However, the thing that adds the greatest intrigue to this story for me is that some biblical scholars argue that the Kopet Dag Mountains are the true location of the Garden of Eden. According to them, it was not an apple that eve plucked, but a wild pomegranate

MELON

One day in 2004, the then-Turkemen President Saparmurat Niyazov spoke to Turkmen farmers in Ashgabat and said, "Almighty God has turned Turkmen soil into a fertile source of an abundance of the tastiest fruits. Among them are Turkmen melons". That day was a national holiday, named "Melon Day"

The holiday was established in 1994 by Niyazov (or "Turkmenbashi", as he preferred to be called), and was set up to celebrate the melon in all its many forms, but especially the "Turkmenbashi Melon" a crossbred muskmelon famed for its size and richness of flavour.

The largest celebrations are in Ashgabat where there is dancing and music to go along with the festivities and the event takes place on the second Sunday of August every year.

Melon day shows Turkmenistan's pride with regard to their melons. Once a major supplier of melons to the Soviet Union, many believe that Turkmenistan has produced 400 varieties of melon (a quarter of the world's 1600 varieties). If that wasn't enough, Turkmen melons have received glowing reviews from Ibn Battutah, a great Arab traveller, and Zahiruddin Muhammad Babur, the founder of the Maghul Empire.

Interesting fact! Egyptian hieroglyphics featuring melons date back to as far as 2400 BC. It was seen as a source of portable water.

ASTANA

ASTANA, KAZAKHSTAN

Astana feels like a science fiction city. Having replaced Almaty in 1997 as the new capital of Kazakhstan, billions of dollars have been poured into its development, resulting in architectural feats such as the symbolic Baiterek tower.

This swift relocation has meant that a whole swathe of jobs have become available in Astana, attracting people in their thousands (both from Kazakhstan and from further afield) to this once sleepy steppe town.

Parks, cafes and restaurants are now emerging all the time. Since the vast majority of the city has been built from scratch in the not-too-distant past, Astana's culinary direction is very much still being established. In an attempt to appeal to an international audience, the capital's restaurants provide a smorgasbord of cuisine from Russia, Central Asia, Europe, China and Korea. It is hoped that Astana represents a new dawn for Kazakhstan, and armed with a keen palette, you might find out what that tastes like.

OKROSHKA

This healthy Russian soup tends to be served in summer because of its refreshing, light taste. Okroshka can be made with kefir (a light yoghurt), water, vinegar, kvass or even beer. Don't be surprised to see some locals adding ice cubes to their portions of Okroshka; that the soup is chilled is of the utmost importance.

Ingredients
70g sour cream
3 tbsp vinegar
2 tsp salt
3 tbsp dill, chopped
220g green onion
220g ham
3-4 potatoes
3 eggs
3-4 small cucumbers

Serves: 8-10 portions

Method
Peel the potatoes and dice them into small cubes. Put them in a medium pot and cover with water. Add a tablespoon of vinegar and bring to a boil. Continue to boil until the potatoes are cooked (about 10 minutes), before draining well and setting aside to cool.

While the potatoes are cooking, boil 3 eggs before cooling them in ice water. Dice the eggs, the cucumbers, and the ham. Chop the dill and the green onions. Mix everything together in a large pot.

In a separate large bowl, whisk 2 litres of cold water together with the sour cream, vinegar and salt until everything is mixed. Pour the mixture into the pot with the rest of ingredients. Chill, and stir well before serving.

KESPE

Kespe is a Kazakh meat and noodle soup. The dish is a staple of Kazakh cuisine and is particularly popular during the brutal Astana winters. I am also told it is a meal that sets a person on the road to recovery when they have a cold.

Ingredients
130g beef or mutton (brisket)
120g onion
3g garlic
1g ground red pepper
240g wheat flour
6 eggs
Vegetable oil
Salt

Serves: 4 portions

Method

Cut the meat into small cubes and fry in vegetable oil in a deep pan. Add salt, pepper and add enough water to cover. Boil the ingredients together until they are soft.

Prepare thick dough by mixing the flour, eggs, a pinch of salt and a little water, before kneading until soft. Allow the dough to sit for 30 to 40 minutes. Roll the dough out into a thin sheet and slice into thin strips to make noodles.

Boil the noodles and layer on the bottom of serving bowls. Ladle the meat and broth over the noodle, and sprinkle the mixture with greens for decoration.

KUKSI

Kuksi is a dish made popular in Kazakhstan by the Koryo Saram (ethnic Koreans living in post-Soviet states). It is a dish that perfectly illustrates how the culinary traditions that were imported with the Koreans have blended with local produce. Korean food is a hit in Astana, and Kuksi is the star.

Ingredients

650-950g lean meat, sliced into thin strips (beef works well in Kuksi)
Oil, 5 medium onions, thinly sliced
4 medium tomatoes, Salt (to taste)
Ground pepper (to taste)
5 cloves garlic, Cilantro (to taste)
1 cabbage, thinly sliced
2 cucumbers, thinly sliced
Radishes, diced (amount optional)
Soy sauce (to taste), 4 eggs
Hot peppers, thinly sliced (amount optional)
1 pack spaghetti
Kuksi Muri (Kuksi Broth) – Hot or Cold
1l water, 2 tbsp sugar
1 tbsp salt, 1 tsp white vinegar
1 tbsp of a rich soy sauce
Tomatoes, diced (optional)
Serves: 8 portions

Method

Fry meat under cover to soften (10 minutes). Add 2 sliced onions, and simmer until onions become translucent. Add 2 sliced tomatoes and stir regularly until the ingredients are cooked. Salt to taste, allow mixture to sit for a few minutes and add ground pepper and 2 cloves of crushed garlic.

Sprinkle sliced cabbage with salt and toss. Fry 2 sliced onions in oil until they are golden. Add 2 chopped tomatoes and simmer. Meanwhile, rinse the cabbage and squeeze out as much water as possible. Add the cabbage and stir fry over medium heat (retaining its crunch). Remove from heat. Add cilantro, black pepper and 3-4 cloves of crushed garlic. Set aside.

Season 2 sliced cucumbers with fried onions, garlic, black pepper, cilantro and a soy sauce. Set aside. Toss diced radishes with salt. After 10 minutes, rinse radishes, squeeze out the water and season with fried onions, garlic, black pepper, cilantro and soy sauce. Set aside. Hard-boil the eggs and cut them in half. Set aside.

Fry some sliced onion, and add tomatoes, then hot peppers. Cover and simmer (10 minutes). Uncover and fry until cooked and the pepper skins have softened. Season with garlic and pepper.

Cook the spaghetti. As soon as it has cooked, [r]under cold water and drain. Make spaghetti [nest]s and leave to harden. Place spaghetti nests [in e]ach bowl and layer the different salads on [top] before pouring on Kuksi Muri (made by simply [mixing] the Kusi Muri ingredients).

BAKU

BAKU, AZERBAIJAN

Baku is an exciting, eclectic city, where east, west, old and new have all found their place. The medieval fortress wall of Baku's Old City (**İçəri Şəhər**) separates ancient and UNESCO listed buildings such as the Palace of the Shirvanshahs and Maiden Tower, with immaculately maintained parks, pedestrian walkways and the city's ultra-modern oil-rich business district. Lada's, a distinctly Soviet phenomenon, buzz around architectural fusions influenced by the Ottomans, Persians and Arabs.

As the largest city on the Caspian, and as a metropolis that seems to be expanding exponentially, the restaurants of the "City of Winds" now have a worldwide audience to which they can serve Azerbaijani delicacies.

The food, much like the city itself, reflects many centuries of cultural influence from Persia, Turkey and the Soviet Union, and incorporates fruits, vegetables, herbs and spices from the 9 distinct climate zones that are packed into this Caucasian nation.

15

SHIRIN PLOV

Plov (or pilaf) is ubiquitous in Azerbaizani cuisine, but shirin plov (meaning "sweet pilaf") is distinctive. It is served with sweet dried fruits like raisins or apricots, and, as with many plovs, is also served with a qazmaq (a dough crust). Many locals in Baku consider shirin plov to be the king of Azerbaijani pilafs.

Ingredients
400g basmati rice
200g butter
2 tbsp saffron infusion
3 tbsp salt
1 flour tortilla (to use as a qazmaq - optional)
1 cup dried Apricots
1 cup raisins

Method

Take half a teaspoon of dried saffron threads and toss them into a glass with two tablespoons of boiling water, turning the water orange.

In a saucepan, melt two tablespoons of butter, add two tablespoons of hot water, add the dried apricots (cut them in half if they are too large) and add the raisins. Simmer over low heat for a few minutes until they are plump. Stir constantly.

Boil the rice with a little salt. The rice should be hard on the inside and soft on outside. Drain, and set it aside.

Mix most of the dried fruit with the rice in a bowl, but save some for garnishing. Melt two tablespoons of butter into a saucepan and set the qazmaq (your tortilla) on top of the butter. Spread roughly a quarter of the rice on top and pour on 2-3 tablespoons of melted butter. Repeat this buttered layering with all your rice. On the last layer, pour on your saffron infusion with some butter. Make some air holes in the rice and cover. Cook over low heat for (60 minutes).

Serve on a large plate and garnish with fruit.

STURGEON SHASHLIK WITH NARSHARAB

Sturgeon is fished fresh from the Caspian, and there is no better way to enjoy it than grilled with the Azerbaijani pomegranate sauce, narsharab, prepared by one of Baku's master chefs. Note however, that though historically sturgeon has been a treat for many along the Caspian coast in Azerbaijan, recent research suggests that fish stocks are being depleted as a result of overfishing. Bear this in mind.

Ingredients
450g sturgeon fillet, skinless
30g sour cream
1 onion
1 bunch spring onions
Vegetable oil
Narsharab (tangy pomegranate sauce)
Pinch of sumac
Salt, pepper (to taste)

Serves: 5-6 portions

Method
Wash the sturgeon and pat dry. Cut fish into 3cm cubes and sprinkle with salt and pepper before coating in sour cream.

Thread the cubes of fish onto long skewers and cook over a hot grill for 7 to 10 minutes, turning regularly.

Serve the fish as soon as it is cooked, accompanied by raw sliced onion, chopped spring onions and fresh, sliced tomato. Serve the narsharab and sumac in separate bowls from the rest of the dish.

SULU KHINGAL

Sulu Khingal is a traditional Azerbaijani dish that can be served both as a starter, and as a main course. The soup is given its distinctive taste through the use of fresh herbs. While the recipe below represents a good starting point for this dish, variants can be found all over Baku and Azerbaijan.

Ingredients
250g lamb (or beef)
1 small onion
1 tbsp butter
1 cup canned chickpeas (or soak and cook your own for extra freshness!)
A pinch of turmeric
Salt, grape vinegar and mint (to taste)
2 cups flour
1 egg
1 tsp salt

Method
Make dough from the egg, salt and water, and knead until it is soft and elastic. Shape the dough into a ball, cover with cling film, and set aside for 20 minutes. Roll out the dough on a floured surface into a large thin layer, and cut it into small squares.

Slice the meat into small pieces, cover with water and bring to a boil. When boiling, skim the foam off, and add the chickpeas, turmeric and salt to taste. Simmer until the meat is cooked. Meanwhile, cut the onion into small pieces and fry in a butter until golden brown.

As soon as the meat is cooked, add the squares of dough to the broth, gently mix them with a spoon, lower the heat, and simmer until the dough is tender (5 minutes).

Decorate each serving bowl of Sulu Khingal with chopped mint and the fried onion. Serve vinegar as a side.

QATIG QOVURMA PLOV

Apparently, qatig qovurma plov (or "yogurt pilaf") is unique in Azerbaijani cuisine, originating from the ancient Iravan Khanate. I have been led to believe that the exact recipe is only known by those in Baku who have had it passed down to them through the generations. Baku's chefs have let one thing slip though: if you want fluffy, soft rice for this plov (or any plov for that matter), soak the rice overnight in salty water before cooking.

Ingredients
400g basmati rice
3 tbsp salt
250g unsalted butter
2 tbsp saffron infusion
1 flour tortilla (for qazmaq - optional)
900g plain yogurt (qatig)
700 g lean lamb or beef
1 large onion, Salt and pepper (to taste)
tsp saffron threads

Serves: 3-4 portions

Method
Cube the meat. Cook the meat in 2 tablespoons of butter over medium-high heat until lightly brown on all sides. Peel the onion, and slice into half-rings. Mix the onion and the meat together. Lower the heat and cover, and allow to simmer. As soon as the meat begins releasing juice, season it with salt and pepper, and continue to simmer until the meat is cooked. Stir occasionally.

Drain the yoghurt through a double layer of cheesecloth for 6 hours. What is left will look like cottage cheese. Squeeze any extra moisture out and transfer into a saucepan. Add saffron threads and stir well. Cook over low heat while constantly stirring, until it begins to steam and bubble. Add cooked meat, stir, and simmer over low heat (15 minutes).

Prepare the saffron infusion, boil the rice, layer with butter (include qazmaq) and cook on a low heat in a process like that of shirin pilaf. Serve the meat over the rice and garnish.

KHAZAR SALAD

"Khazar" is Azerbaijani for "Caspian", and the khazar salad gets its name because it incorporates the finest bounty the Caspian has to offer. This dish combines sturgeon, salmon and black and red caviar, unsurprisingly making it one of the most expensive salads on the planet. Unfortunately, it is not great for the local ecosystem.

Ingredients
3 potatoes
3 fresh cucumbers
A few sprigs of tarragon
2 tbsp sour cream
1 tbsp mayonnaise
Salt and pepper (to taste)
Fillet of fresh sturgeon
5-6 slices of smoked salmon
Red and/or black caviar
1 lettuce
1 lemon
1 cucumber

Method

Slice the fillet of fresh sturgeon, place in a saucepan with cold water, and bring it to a boil over medium heat. Skim the broth as necessary, add salt and pepper, and simmer until tender (20 minutes). Set aside to cool.

Wash the potatoes, place them in a pot with cold water and bring the water to a boil. Simmer until they are soft (about 30 minutes). Allow the potato to cool, and then peel off the skins.

Cut the potatoes and cucumbers into medium size cubes and mix together with tarragon leaves, sour cream, and mayonnaise in a bowl. Season with salt and pepper to taste.

Place the lettuce leaves of green lettuce on a serving plate and layer with the potato-cucumber mixture. Decorate with pieces of sturgeon, and thin, rolled slices of smoked salmon filled with caviar. Garnish with sliced lemon, cucumber, and sprigs of tarragon.

MILK PILAF RECIPE

Südlü pilaf can be eaten on its own or served with smoked fish for a pleasing contrast between sweet and savoury.

Ingredients
1 glass of rice
1 1/2 glasses of milk
75-100 g/3-4 oz of unsalted butter
50-75 g/2-3 oz of golden raisins
10 dates
5 dried apricots, separated in half (optional)
a few strands of saffron
2 teaspoons of sugar (optional)
pinch of salt

Method
Put a few threads of saffron in a cup and add boiling water. Cover and leave to infuse.

Rinse the dried fruit.

Wash the rice and drain well.

Put the rice in a saucepan and add the milk, butter, salt and saffron infusion. Put the pan on a low flame.

Simmer until almost all the milk has been absorbed by the rice. When some two-thirds of the milk has been absorbed, add the dried fruit.

Place a well-fitting lid on top of the saucepan, covered underneath with a clean tea towel. The towel helps to absorb the steam. Turn the heat down as low as possible and leave the rice to finish cooking.

ISKENDER KEBAB

You might be thinking, "Hang on, isn't that Turkish?", and given that the dish takes its name from its Turkish creator, Iskender Efendi, you would be right. The fact that a dish so quintessentially Turkish has gained such popularity in Azerbaijan's capital says a lot about the extent of the cultural influence exerted from the west. Make sure you order this with a frothing glass of Ayran.

Ingredients
450g beef tenderloin/steak
4 medium tomatoes
2 green chili peppers
1 cup tomato sauce (or can of crushed tomatoes)
2 tbsp of melted butter
Salt, pepper and garlic (to taste)
3-4 pieces pita bread
Yogurt

Method
Season the meat with salt and pepper and fry with butter on medium-high heat. Leave in the pan when done.

Turn your grill to medium-high heat (or preheat the oven to 205°C). Cut tomatoes in half and grill with the chili peppers. Put canned tomato sauce in a saucepan, add salt, pepper, one tablespoon of butter and two finely chopped roasted tomatoes. Cook over low heat (5 minutes).

Take the meat out of the pan, and slice it as thin as possible. Place pieces of meat back in the frying pan and mix well with the residual juice.

Crush the garlic, and mix into the yogurt with salt. Mix well.

Warm up the pita and cut into diamonds before layering on plate. Spread the meat evenly over the layer of pita. Pour the tomato sauce on top and place a few spoons of yogurt on the side. Garnish with the grilled tomatoes and chili peppers.

BISHKEK

CHUY PROVINCE, KYRGYZSTAN

Though incomparable to Almaty or Tashkent in terms of sheer global reach, Bishkek's food scene is nonetheless packed with intrigue.

Set up as a Khokand fortress on a branch of the Silk Road that weaved its way west through the Tian Shan, Bishkek's purpose was to generate donations from Kyrgyz clans that passed through. Nearly two hundred years later, it seems to me that culinary donations are still flooding in from Kyrgyz people across the land.

Bishkek still has the feel of a city trying to find its place in the world, and while it is certainly doing so, it is precisely because of this that its history can be read from its menus. Traditional foods, as well as Russian, Uygur and now Korean, are aplenty.

KYRGYZ KUURDAK

Kuurdak is one of Kyrgyzstans oldest dishes and its name refers to the way the dish is prepared. It was particularly useful for the nomads because it allowed them to cook, store and transport the meat, ready to be eaten at a later time. Though Kuurdak was originally made from organs, it is much more common to see beef or lamb used today. In Bishkek, you might even see new world ingredients like potatoes being incorporated. Either way, Kuurdak is simple and delicious.

Ingredients
900g meat (beef, lamb or mutton) cut into small chunks, 4 onions, peeled and sliced
120ml cup vegetable oil
3 green bell peppers, seeded and julienned
Handful of julienned cabbage
1/2 tsp ground red pepper
1/2 tsp black pepper, 1 tsp salt, 2 bay leaves
2 tbsp tomato paste

Method
Fry the meat in vegetable oil for 10 to 15 minutes until brown. Add sliced onion, green peppers, cabbage, ground red pepper, black pepper, salt, bay leaves, water, and tomato paste.

Add about half a litre of water and partially cover the pan and allow the mixture to simmer for roughly 35 to 45 minutes, until the water has been absorbed and the ingredients are soft. Drain, remove the bay leaves, and serve the meat hot together with the vegetables.

MAKSYM

Maksym, much like jarma, is a beverage created from barley, wheat or corn. Folklore has it that in the mid-1800s, the wife of Urumbai Khan added yeast to jarma and allowed it to ferment. This made jarma alcoholic, and thus Maksym was born. The nomads believed that their new drink would give them the strength to work during the long and blisteringly hot summer days in the mountains. One sip, and you can understand why.

Maksym was actually the first drink to be sold by Shoro after the collapse of the Soviet Union in 1992. Initially, the beverage was sold fresh from the keg in Bishkek's Dordoi Bazaar, and this heritage has been carried forward by the company. As you stroll down Bishkek's wide, leafy boulevards, you will still see Shoro (and now Enesay) vendors sitting on every major intersection. If you ask nicely in Kyrgyz or Russian, they might even give you a free taster.

BUKHARA

BUKHARA PROVINCE, UZBEKISTAN

If you want to experience pre-Russian Turkestan, lose yourself in Bukhara with a hot alat samsa in hand. The breath-taking Old Town of Bukhara is packed with colourful madrassas and mosques, some of which have a history that goes back an entire millennium. By most accounts, the city itself is roughly 2,500 years old, and the area around it has been inhabited for around 5000 years.

Given the sheer amount of time the city has been in existence, and given its strategic importance on the Silk Road, it shouldn't be surprising that Bukhara has an incredible history of trade, merging cultures and religious exchange. Dozens of groups of people, from the Persians to the Bukharan Jews, have influenced the cuisine of this ancient city, and evidence is not hard to come by.

BAKHSH

Ingredients:
1 kg rice
500 g. lamb or beef,
300 g. mutton or beef liver,
2 large onions,
300 g. sheep fat,
2 bunches of cilantro,
100 ml vegetable oil
salt and black pepper

Method

A meat cubes 1x1 cm are thoroughly roasted in the hot oil. The liver and fat of sheep's tail are chopped the same way. They are added to the meat and everything is mixed. Immediately seductive smell appears, but we can not relax. It is necessary to put sliced onion (half rings) and finely chopped cilantro to a meat (onions are often mixed with soaking rice, and it goes in Bakhsh last). Mix everything and add water to it so that it covers the contents. The heat must be such, so that all is bubbling, and zirvak, which Uzbeks call all ingredients used before we add rice, is boiled. The heat can be reduced: the longer zirvak is cooked, the better it tastes. By the way, Italians say the same, when they do salsa. Soak rice in advance and add to zirvak. Pour a little water, salt and stir until the water goes into the rice – the heat must be high. Gather rice in knoll, cover the cauldron, remove the heat to low and Bakhsh is ready in a half and hour. Bakhsh is loved by everybody even those who can not stand cilantro. For baksh in the bag ingredients are mixed and filled a bag available in every Bukharan family. It is necessary to leave some space in for the swollen rice after it tied up. But after the rice is swelled, there should not left any space. Pouch brewed 2-2.5 hours during cooking flips more content falls in lyagan - wide dish and serve. The bag is boiled for 2-2.5 hours, it is turned over during cooking, then the contents are got out on lyagan - wide dish. Then it can be served.

CHAKKA SALAD

Suzma - Sour milk (yogurt) is laid out in gauze, folded several times, and suspended for a few hours. In two hours Chakka will be thinner, in four hours - more densely. A mass-like liquid curd is left after whey is drained in a gauze. This is Syuzma-Chakka. We do not need to cook it in Uzbekistan, since it is sold in the dairies in any markets. It is served as an appetizer.

Ingredients:
Suzma - 500 g
Scallion - 2 bunches
Cilantro - 1/2 bunch
Dill - 1/2 bunch
Basil - 1 sprig
Radishes - 4-5
Onion - 1
Cucumber - 1
Salt and spices - To taste

Method

Wash in cold water scallions, basil, cilantro, and dill. Finely chop everything. Mix suzma with drinking water to get sour cream consistency, season with salt, ground caraway seeds, and pepper. Mix prepared greens with suzma and transfer to a salad bowl. If desired -- add sliced radishes and cucumbers. Alternatively -- carve "bowls" from onions and serve salad in those bowls.

ALAT SAMSA

For dough:
flour 1 ½ kg
warm water 3 ½ glass
salt 1 teaspoon
sugar — 1 teaspoon
1 egg
Vegetable oil — ½ glass

For a filling:
Minced pumpkin 1 kg
finely -chopped onion
fresh beef, once passed through
a meat grinder — 100 g.
Vegetable oil — 1/3 glass
salt
pepper

Cooking the filling:

Heat the oil in a saucepan and fry the onion until is becomes gold yellow. Add meat and fry until it is brown. Add the pumpkin and mix. Add 2 tablespoons of water, salt and pepper. Stir and cook until it boils. Cook over low heat for about half an hour, until the liquid has evaporated. Stir from time to time, in order the filling does not burn slightly. Cooking the dough: knead the dough making of all the ingredients in a large bowl and let the dough be right in a 1 and a half or two hours. Make 6 balls, knead well each ball and leave the dough for half an hour to be right again. Roll out each ball using a floured rolling pin. From time to time, sprinkle it with flour to make the dough not sticky. With the help of a teaspoon lay out portions of the fillings onto a dough sheet with an interval of 10 cm. Spread the filling only on one half of the dough. Cover the filling of the second half of the sheet. Cut the dough with circular toothed blade into triangles and rectangle. Carefully move on floured tray. Heat in a pan with oil and gently deep fry the samosas. The dough should absorb the oil and increase in volume. Fry until it is light brown.

DUSHANBE

REGION OF REPUBLICAN SUBORDINATION, TAJIKISTAN

Dushanbe is the attractive capital of Tajikistan. Its chilled vibe, serene mountain surroundings and tree-lined streets give it that Sunday afternoon feel, which is ironic because "Dushanbe" actually means "Monday" in Tajik.

The reason for this is that after the Tajik Soviet Socialist Republic was created in 1929, the city grew rapidly from a village that was renowned for its exceptionally popular Monday market.

Dushanbe's chefs have harnessed and refined many of the culinary tradtions from Tajikistan's semi-nomadic peoples, resulting in the provision of dishes like the famous qurutob (p.72). Though much of Tajikistan's cuisine is shared with its Central Asian neighbours, the distinct taste of its food arises from unique food preparation techniques and ingredient variations resulting from the nation's geography; the full spectrum of which can be experienced in Dushanbe.

But it is not just about the food; it is about the event of eating. Take a seat on a sufa around a Tajik dastarkhan (eating place) to be introduced to a whole new relationship with food.

QURUTOB

While Tajiks talk about both plov and qurutob being national dishes, qurutob is specifically Tajik in a way that plov is not. Qurutob is really a combination of central Asian tastes, using both qurut and fatir in the creation of the dish. Making everything the traditional way is certainly difficult in a western context (though not impossible), which is all the more reason to calibrate your taste buds by sampling this delight in its cultural home.

Ingredients
1 lamb shank (about 650g)
1/2 tsp salt, 1/4 tsp ground cumin
1/4 tsp ground coriander
1/8 tsp chili pepper
50ml olive oil, 450g tomatoes, quartered
200g onions, finely sliced
Salt, 4 qurut balls (about 30g each)
1/2 fatir, 2 tsp parsley chiffonade
2 tsp basil chiffonade

Method
Mix the salt, cumin, coriander, and chili pepper in a container. Season the lamb shank thoroughly with this mixture.

Sauté the meat in oil over a high heat. Add the tomatoes, cover, and cook in a 150°C oven (2½ hours). Uncover, and cook for another 30 minutes, flipping the shank halfway through. Set aside for 10 minutes.

Take the meat from the bones in large chunks and remove the skin from the tomatoes. Pour the residual juice in container and set aside.

In a pan sauté the onions with olive oil over medium heat. Season with salt, and stir regularly until golden. Crumble the qurut into the pan, add the saved juices and 60ml water, then simmer for a couple minutes, stirring constantly. Tear the fatir into small squares, and toss into the pan to soak up the flavour.

Arrange the meat and tomatoes on the fatir in a deep dish. If necessary, reheat in a 150°C oven for 5 minutes. Top with the parsley and basil. Eat with your fingers.

CHEBUREKI

Served as an appetiser, main or a snack, chebureki are either deep fried or baked beef dumplings found in Tajikistan. Interestingly, there are foods very similar in other parts of the former Soviet Union, particularly among the Crimean Tatar diasporas, and so Chebureki serves as a delicious reminder of Tajikistan's common history with many other, far-flung places in the former USSR.

Ingredients
300g flour
4 tbsp olive oil
1 tsp vodka (optional)
1/2 tsp white sugar
450g ground beef
1/2 onion (medium, finely chopped)
6 tbsp milk
Vegetable oil
Salt and pepper (to taste)

Serves: 7 portions

Method
In a large bowl, sift together sugar, salt (about 1/3 teaspoon) and flour. Add olive oil and vodka and about 120ml water (a little at a time) and knead the dough until it is soft. Set aside.

Mix together ground beef, chopped onion and parsley. Season the mixture with salt and pepper and stir in milk to create the filling.

On a lightly floured surface, roll the dough until it is roughly 3mm thick. Cut circles (the size of a tea plate) from it until there is no dough remaining.

Place 2 tablespoons of the filling on one half of the circles, leaving a 1cm space to the edges. Fold and pinch the edges firmly together. Make sure there is no air inside.

In a large frying pan, heat the oil (should cover about half of a cheburek), reduce heat and put in 3 or 4 chebureki. Deep fry on both sides until evenly brown (5 minutes per side).

Allow to drain on paper towels, and serve while hot.

LAVS

Lavs is the local name for sesame halva in Tajikistan, and can include both hard and soft versions of this traditional sweet. You can buy some mouth-watering home-made lavs from the green bazaar (Shah Mansur) in Dushanbe or, failing that, it is easy enough to make yourself.

Ingredients
1 egg white
280g sugar
Juice ½ lemon or ¼ tsp citric acid
Flavourings (vanilla, coffee, chocolate, cardamom etc. – whatever you please)
340g tahini, beaten to mix in any separated oil
Nuts (optional, but pistachios work well for this)

Method
Boil the sugar and 100ml water together with flavourings to a "hard ball" syrup (125°C). Beat the egg white until it forms soft peaks. Gradually add the hot sugar syrup, beating continuously (do this in a light metal bowl, so that you don't cool the syrup too much).

Add toasted nuts if you want to include them (they should be warm from the oven). Warm the tahini to about 50°C, and fold it into the hot sugar foam. Keep folding gently until the mixture gets too stiff to work.

Pack into suitable containers, cover to exclude moisture, and let the halva rest in a cool place for at least a night.

JIZZAKH

JIZZAKH PROVINCE, UZBEKISTAN

Strategically sitting on the fringes of the massive Hunger Steppe and close to Timur's Gate, a narrow pass between the Turkestan and Nurata mountain ranges, Jizzakh used to control the passage to Samarkand, Bukhara and the Zeravshan Valley.

In the middle ages, the region around Jizzakh produced all manner of fabrics, cloths jewellery and metals, and was booming with international Silk Road trade. After being conquered by the Arabs, Jizzakh operated primarily as a place where the sedentary farmers could trade goods and ideas with the roaming nomads that passed through the region.

Like many of the Central Asian cities embroiled in the history of the Silk Road, Jizzakh has been levelled and rebuilt countless times; leaving little trace of the city's eventful and distant past. Luckily, food offers access to some of this heritage and Jizzakh dishes gilmindi and jiz-biz are renowned for their quality in Uzbekistan.

JIZ-BIZ

Many of the more traditional Jizzakh chefs will prepare jiz-biz by utilising special cooking methods to fry organs like liver, lungs, heart and innards in a specific order. It is definitely a dish for meat-lovers, but something everyone (except perhaps the vegetarians among you) should try at least once. For ease of cooking, the recipe I have provided is a simplified version using lamb or cow liver.

Ingredients
450g lamb or cow liver
1 large onion
4 potatoes
4 tbsp unsalted butter
Salt and pepper (to taste)

Serves: 2

Method

Peel the onion and slice it into thin half-rings. Melt two tablespoons of unsalted butter in a frying pan over medium heat and sauté the onion until lightly brown.

Cut the liver into pieces (about 2cm cubes) and add them to the frying pan. Fry and the contents of the pan over medium heat, stirring regularly, until the liver chunks become golden brown on all sides. Add salt and pepper just before the liver is ready.

Peel, wash, and dry the potatoes, before chopping them into small chunks (roughly the same size as the liver chunks). Melt two tablespoons of unsalted butter in a separate pan over medium heat and fry the potatoes until they're golden brown. Add salt once they are ready.

Transfer the potatoes, the liver and the onion into the same pan mix together. Serve while hot.

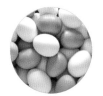

GILMINDI

A recipe native to Jizzakh region, this treasure will keep you full for hours. Though it strikes me as something you might eat as an appetiser or a side, my Uzbek friends insist that it can be eaten as a main. Whichever position it occupies, I am confident you will enjoy this sweet dish.

Ingredients
1 kg flour
750ml milk
2 tbsp sugar
300g butter
Salt

Method
Make sauce by adding 120g flour and 2 tablespoons sugar to milk and boil together until it thickens.

To make dough, add 400ml water and salt to the rest of the sifted flour. Allow to stand in warm place. Cut the dough into 50g pieces, roll out to medium thickness and fry in butter. Coat the top with the milk sauce and fold into a half-moon shape.

KARAKOL

ISSYK-KUL, KYRGYZSTAN

Initially a Russian military outpost founded on the eastern shore of the endless Issyk-Kul and framed by the jagged white peaks of the Tian Shan, Karakol offers the perfect jumping-off point for those after an adventure. If you couple the town's geography with sights like the animal bazaar that is open on Sundays and the wooden Orthodox Church built without nails by the Dungans, it is clear that Karakol offers something distinctly different.

Historically, the region has been subject to influence by the Russians and the Uyghur diaspora, but in the 1880s, the town's culinary profile changed drastically as its population exploded with Dungans who had fled from violence in their native western china. Bringing with them special blends of spices (such as tyochoe), innovative cooking techniques and an array of new rice and noodle dishes, Karakol's new settlers began to exert their influence in the kazan. Today, Dungan, Uyghur and Russian dishes are widely available, sitting comfortably on the menus of Karakol's restaurants alongside local delicacies like Chabak.

ISSYK-KUL FRIED TROUT

With Karakol being almost touching distance from Issyk-Kul, the freshness of the trout is second to none. However, Issyk-Kul has been generally overfished in recent times, and this has resulted in a biodiversity crisis in the lake, and the trout population has been negatively affected.

Ingredients
400-500g trout
150g flour
100-150ml vegetable oil
2 onions
5-6 tomatoes
2 radishes
3-4 sweet peppers
100ml tomato paste
4-5 squashes
Green peas, salt, spices (optional, to taste)

Method
Scale the fish, wash it and cut into slices. Coat the cuts of fish in flour and fry.

Blanch the radish and fry together with the onions. Slice the sweet peppers into strips and mix well with tomato paste before adding to the radish and onion.

Once the fish has cooked, it should be sprinkled with the spices and vegetables, and left to simmer for 5-10 minutes so the flavours can mingle.

Before serving, the dish should be decorated with peas, tomatoes and squashes.

UYGHUR LAGHMAN

The Uyghurs brought their laghman from western China, and it is a dish that has exploded in popularity in Karakol. The primary difference from other versions of this dish is in the way the noodles are prepared, with the dough being delicately pulled and stretched by master Uyghur chefs. This takes a lot of practice to get right, so the recipe here uses a much simpler technique.

Ingredients
120g flour, 1½ tsp salt
2 eggs, 120g cup butter
900g meat (lamb or beef)
4 cups onion, thinly sliced
4 cups potato, cubed
2 cups carrots, thinly sliced
4 cups tomatoes, sliced
1/4 cup garlic, minced
2 cups red bell peppers,
seeded and thinly sliced
6 cups cabbage, thinly sliced
1 tbsp salt
2 tsp pepper

Method
Whisk together 120ml water and the eggs before mixing this with the flour and salt until dough forms. Knead the dough on a flat, floured surface for about 10 minutes until the dough becomes soft. Roll the dough out and cut into thin strips before boiling for two minutes. Remove the noodles when ready, rinse and drain.

To make the tudzuk (soup), melt the butter in a large pot over medium heat, then sauté the onions until they turn golden. Add the meat and fry a little before adding the potatoes, carrots, tomatoes, garlic and red bell peppers. Stir frequently, until the vegetables are half-cooked. Stir in the cabbage, salt and pepper and add about 4 litres of water. Bring to a boil and allow the mixture to simmer until the vegetables are cooked through.

Heat the noodles and serve them in bowls before ladling the tudzuk on top. Serve hot.

ASHLAM FU

Ashlam fu is a kind of spicy, cold noodle broth made with vegetables and corn starch. This dish is one of the most popular Dungan imports to Kyrgyzstan, and has a special place in the kitchens of those in Karakol, many of whom have Dungan heritage. You will notice many specialist Dungan restaurants in Karakol, and most serve fantastic ashlam fu.

Ingredients
50g rice or corn starch
300g flour
100g vegetable oil
3-4 eggs
2 onions
1 clove garlic
2-3 tomatoes
2 tbsp vinegar
2-3 leeks
2-3 green peppers
Dill, chili and salt (to taste)

Method
Make thin noodles from flour eggs water and a touch of salt (slightly thinner than those of Uyghur Laghman)

Dissolve starch in 350ml water, boil and pour onto a flat dish. When the starch thickens and cools, cut it into strips. Pour the egg into a cup with a little oil, whisk and boil in water.

Fry onion, garlic, chopped leek, green peppers and tomatoes in a deep pan, add salt and mix together. When the ingredients have cooked, add roughly 650ml of water and bring to a boil. Allow the mixture to simmer and the flavours to mix before removing it from heat and allowing it to cool.

Put noodles and boiled egg in serving bowls with the chopped starch and pour soup on top. Add vinegar and herbs to taste.

MAMPAR

I am informed that Mampar is a traditional Uyghur dish, though its exact origins are uncertain. However, many of Karakol's restaurants offer this excellent dumpling soup. Be careful, sometimes mampar can be very spicy.

Ingredients
1kg (with bones)
2 sweet peppers
4 tomatoes
2 bulbs
3 cloves garlic
6 hot peppers (1 per serving)
2 eggs
1 cup flour
Fresh basil (to taste)
3 tbsp vegetable oil
A pinch of cumin

Serves: 6 portions

Method
Sift the flour into a bowl and add 1 egg. Knead the dough and let it stand for 20-30 minutes.

From dough, form small dumplings and boil. Once the dumplings float, drain, add a little oil and set aside.

Whisk an egg and fry gently to make a thin pancake. Cut pancake into small pieces and set aside.

Dice the meat and slice the onion, tomatoes, peppers and garlic. Fry pepper and garlic for roughly 2 minutes on high heat, before putting aside.

Fry the meat in a deep pan until brown. Add onion and cook until transparent. Add chopped tomatoes, stir and simmer on low heat for about 15 minutes. Add 3 litres of boiling water, and simmer for roughly 40 minutes. Add hot pepper to taste. Once nearly done, add garlic and pepper, season with salt, a pinch of cumin and fresh basil and remove from heat, letting the soup sit (covered) for 10-15 minutes.

Serve soup over mini-dumplings and decorate with thinly sliced pancake.

BOZO

With its roots in the clans of Kyrgyzstan, Kazakhstan and Tartarstan, this wonderfully-named drink is made by grinding down and boiling barley or corn and adding pounded shoots of the grain in order to ferment the mixture. The alcoholic content of the drink depends on the quantity of shoots added, and can be anywhere between 1 and 9 percent.

Bozo is traditionally consumed by men in the winter to "warm them from the inside", and is thought by many to have medicinal qualities. Locals spoke of its ability to boost levels of vitamin E, and promote red blood cell production. For this reason, it was traditionally offered to women who had just given birth.

Incidentally, Bozo was the last Shoro product to be industrialised because of the complicated nature of its filtration. It was in fact so difficult that workers were filtering the grain husks from the mixture by hand until the late 90s. Eventually, Egemberdiev (the owner of Shoro) visited a food processing plant and realised that he could adapt a mechanical tomato-seeder to do the job.

That you can now buy bozo in supermarkets throughout Kyrgyzstan and beyond is testament to that piece of innovation.

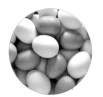

KOKAND

FERGANA PROVINCE, UZBEKISTAN

According to travellers' accounts of the India-China caravan route, Kokand has been around for about a thousand years. But Khokand really made its name in the 18th and 19th century, when it was the capital of a powerful Khanate that ruled throughout the Fergana Valley. At the time, it was considered second only to Bukhara in terms of religious significance, and home to dozens of madrassas and too many mosques to count.

Unfortunately, most of these architectural artefacts are no longer around after the town was sacked by the Tashkent Soviets in the early 1900s. However, considering Kokand was once the cultural epicentre of the region, it is certainly still worth a visit.

The markets in Kokand are excellent, making them a great place to purchase authentic Uzbek sweets like parvarda, navat and nisholda. The meat in the Fergana valley is also excellent, and the quality of Khokand's shashlik is testament to this.

SHASHLIK

Shashlik is a mainstay of Central Asian cuisine, and can be found in every city mentioned in this book, as well as further afield. A simple dish that can be made with beef, chicken, pork, fish and even camel, shashlik is as versatile as it is delicious. The quality of the meat in the Fegana valley is superb, making it the perfect place to try Shashlik.

Ingredients
900g lamb (boneless leg or shoulder is best)
1 onion, thinly sliced
Salt and pepper (to taste)
Juice of 2 lemons
3 tbsp oil

Method
Toss the lamb, onion, salt and pepper, lemon juice and oil together in a large bowl. Cover and refrigerate for at least 2 hours (but preferably overnight) to marinate.

Cut meat into 3cm cubes and thread the chunks onto skewers and grill the meat skewers over the hot flame, turning frequently, until the meat is cooked to your liking.

Serve the skewers with a vegetable salad (achichuk goes well with this), and, if you want to be particularly fancy, slices of rye bread and serve with a fine Uzbek wine.

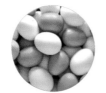

SWEETS

Sweets are an essential part of Uzbek tea-times and national or religious holidays. Though many can be purchased throughout the year at the bazaar, like parvarda or navat, others, such as nisholda or sumalyak, are really only available on special occasions.

Parvarda is a caramel pillow coated in flour, and often there are herbs added to give the sweet a different flavour. Navat, on the other hand, is made from crystallised grape sugar and boiled together with spices that are believed to have medicinal qualities. It is not uncommon to see navat used in folk medicine.

On the eve of Nawruz (cultural holiday), you will see women all over Khokand working tirelessly to prepare nisholda and sumalyak (among other things) for the festivities ahead. Nisholda is made with egg-whites, sugar and herbs, while sumalyak is a sweet paste made in a large pot from germinated wheat. If you are in Khokand for Nawruz, prepare yourself for monstrous offerings of these treats.

KHOROG

GORNO-BADAKHSHAN (GBAO), TAJIKISTAN

A picturesque Pamir-valley town sitting amongst spectacular and angular peaks on the border with Afghanistan, Khorog is the capital of the autonomous Gorno-Badakhshan (GBAO) region in Tajikistan.

For a long time, Khorog was a small settlement that exchanged hands between local chiefs, Afghan Shahs and the Emir of Bukhara. That was until the 1896 Russian-Anglo-Afghan Border Treaty, when the Russians set up a military presence in the town. During Soviet rule, various plants were erected, designed to produce foods (including dairy products), shoes and building materials. Several universities have since been built and the town is now known for the highly educated populous that reside there.

Luckily for us, the dairy industry is still alive and kicking, making Khorog one of the best places to enjoy yoghurt-based tastes qurut and kaymak with non and a steaming pot of tea.

QURUT

Qurut are balls of dried, salted yoghurt. This process of preparation was initially developed by the nomads in order to preserve dairy produce ahead of long journeys. Obviously, it is very difficult for most people to recreate traditional, nomadic Qurut (though I would encourage you to try if you have the necessary livestock!), so I have made sure that this recipe uses ingredients that can be obtained at your average supermarket. You can use them as snacks with tea, as part of other meals, or even to make drinks.

Ingredients
500g plain whole milk yogurt
2.5g salt

Serves: 4 qurut balls of about 30g each

Method
Pour the yogurt into a baking dish, and oven cook for 1½ hours at 150°C. When done, pour the yogurt through a chinois, gently pressing with a spatula to extract more whey. Throw away the liquid.

Mix the solids with the salt, put back on the baking tray, and cook for another 30 minutes.

Remove the yogurt solids from the dish and divide the solids into 4 parts. Squeeze each one to make a tight ball ready to store or serve (or, if you think they are really good, to sell in a Central Asian market!).

KAYMAK

Traditionally, kaymak is made from fresh, unpasteurised cow or sheep milk. When the milk begins to cool, the cream that forms at the top is skimmed off, salted and put in a wooden container. The milk is then boiled, and the process is carried out again. This is repeated over and over to produce a high-fat clotted cream that is served as an appetiser, often alongside flatbread and tea. Here is an easier way:

Ingredients (for "quick" kaymak)
400g sour cream
200g feta cheese
400g softened cream cheese

Serves: 4 portions

Method
Press feta cheese through a sieve and into a large bowl. Add the sour cream and cream cheese, and beat all of the ingredients together until the mixture is smooth.

Refrigerate for a while. Allow the kaymak to get to room temperature before serving.

NON

Popular in cities along the Silk Road and ubiquitous in Central Asia, non is served with many meals, and is cloaked in superstition. Tajiks will often say that they are out of food if they have no accompanying non, and the bread must never be put upside-down or have anything placed on top of it (unless another piece of non) as this brings bad luck. Remember too, that it is tradition for the oldest member present to break the bread first.

Ingredients
1 tsp sugar
1 tbsp dry yeast
1 cup plain yogurt (2 percent or whole milk)
1 tbsp salt
120g whole wheat flour
300-400g all-purpose flour
2 tbsp finely chopped shallot
1 tsp salt

Method

Stir together 100ml warm water, sugar, and yeast in a large bowl. Stir together yogurt and 200ml water in a saucepan over medium heat, until lukewarm. Add this to the yeast and water mixture and stir. Add the whole wheat flour one cup at a time, stirring as you add the flour. Set the mix aside, covered, for upwards of 10 minutes.

Sprinkle 1 tablespoon of salt over the mixture, then stir in all-purpose flour one cup at a time until dough is too stiff to stir. Knead for 10 minutes on a floured surface, until the dough becomes smooth.

Lightly oil the bowl before adding the dough, covering with plastic wrap, and allowing it to rise until it has doubled in volume (1½ hours). Preheat the oven to 260°C. Place dough on a floured surface, and divide into 8 pieces. Roll out each piece into a 15cm round.

With a fork pierce and flatten a 4cm diameter circle at the centre of the bread to prevent it from rising. Sprinkle on □ teaspoon chopped shallot, a pinch of salt, and a sprinkle with water.

Bake until the nons are lightly golden (5-8 minutes). Remove from the oven. Place on a rack to cool.

TEA

A sign of hospitality and brought with every meal and every snack, if ever there was an all-encompassing Central Asian taste, it would have to be tea.

Served in a china pot, and drunk from a piala (a small drinking bowl without a handle), tea is often accompanied by sweets and bread on a traditional Tajik dastarkhan (eating place). It is often consumed with sugar or honey as a sweetener, and both black and green varieties are widely available. Such is the popularity of tea, chaikhanas (tea houses) operate as meeting places and local hangouts, much like cafes or bars in the west.

Given that you can get tea everywhere, there are a number of great places throughout the region that you can slurp on this soothing drink. Khorog, however, offers the unique experience of sipping a brew from a piala amidst the buzz of meeting friends and the famous, razor-sharp Pamir peaks.

Interesting fact!
Long before the 19th century, solid blocks of tea were used as a currency in Siberia

KHUDJAND

SUGHD PROVINCE, TAJIKISTAN

Sitting in the north of Tajikistan, protected by the Fan mountains, is one of the oldest cities in Central Asia: Khujand.

Khujand was actually founded as Alexander the Great's easternmost outpost in the 4th century BC, and went on to generate huge amounts of wealth by controlling the Fergana valley trade routes, and taxing those that wanted to pass. The city was booming, and the controlling powers erected mosques, palaces and a grand citadel, the vast majority of which was destroyed when the Mongols laid waste to the city in the early 13th century.

Khujand has a large Uzbek population, and a reputation for good meat, so trying the shashlik and kebabs must be near the top of your hit-list. Meat, however, is not the only thing you must try. The apricot gardens here produce some of the tastiest apricots in the world (and their blossoms are truly beautiful in the spring) and, of course, let's not forget about the pumpkin sombusas.

PUMPKIN SOMBUSA

Authentic pumpkin sombusa (or samsa) is baked in a tandyr oven (large, clay oven), and offers an interesting alternative to the usually meaty fillings that come in samsas across Central Asia. This is a snack that is delicious, and slightly more nutritious.

Ingredients
300g wheat flour
2g salt
400g pumpkin
80g sheep fat
100g onion
10g ground pepper

Method

In a bowl, mix flour, eggs, salt and a little water to prepare the dough, and knead until soft. Set aside for 30-40 minutes.

Cut the pumpkin and fat into small cubes, add some chopped onion, salt and pepper, and mix everything together well. Set aside

Make small balls out of the dough and roll each ball flat before putting a spoonful of the pumpkin and onion mix in the middle. Fold into a semi-circle.

Bake for 25 to 30 minutes at 200-220°C until golden. Serve hot or cold.

FATIR

Fatir is a unique, flaky, nutritious flatbread that is an integral part of Tajik national dish Qurutob. A bread that is similar to the Indian paratha, it serves as an example of the interconnectedness of various cooking practices throughout the larger Asian continent.

Ingredients

200g flour, sifted
½ tsp salt
30ml water
1 small egg
35g butter, room temperature
35g rendered lamb fat (or just more butter), room temperature
½ tsp sesame seeds

Method

Beat together the flour, salt, 30ml water and the egg, until dough forms. Knead until smooth, and shape the dough into a ball, cover with plastic wrap, and set aside for 30 minutes.

Place a baking dish full of water in an oven set to 230°C. On a floured surface, roll the dough to a 15 by 30cm rectangle. Cut it lengthwise into two long strips.

Mix together the butter and lamb fat, and spread on the dough. Roll the first strip up and wrap the second strip around it to create a fat, two-layered cylinder. Cover with cling-film, and refrigerate for at least 1 hour.

Stand the cylinder of dough on a floured surface and using the palm of your hand gradually flatten the dough into a thick disc. Sprinkle the top and bottom generously with flour.

Prick the flatbread with a fork, creating a decorative pattern, sprinkle the sesame seeds on top, and gently press the seeds into the dough. Transfer onto a baking sheet, and bake until the top is golden brown (25-30 minutes). Allow to rest on a cooling rack before serving.

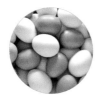

APRICOTS

Apricots are notoriously sweet in the Fergana valley, and by all accounts the aroma of the apricot gardens is something to behold in and of itself. Though there is a rich diversity of the fruit in the Fergana valley, Khujand locals speak particularly highly of a kind named "Kandak".

Kandak apricots are said to grow only in the Khujand region and are apparently the sweetest apricots of them all. It is held in such high esteem here that it is believed to have healing powers, and is actually prescribed by doctors as a natural medicine for people with chronic illness.

The export of fresh and dried fruit is a growing industry in the north of Tajikistan. The apricot has become such a star in this part of the world that in 2013, the Tajik president, Emomali Rahmon, took part in Idi Zardolu (Festival of the Apricot) celebrations that were hosted in Khujand on 19th June.

Interesting fact!

One apricot has only 17 calories. In Latin, the apricot is called praecocquum, which means "early-ripening peach."

LANKARAN

LANKARAN, AZERBAIJAN

In the 18th century, Lankaran was the capital of the Talysh empire, and to this day is home to a Talysh population determined to preserve their ancient customs. In particular, these customs include pottery, sewing, copperware, and of course, food.

Cooking is a skill taken very seriously in the south of Azerbaijan, with methods and techniques being passed from generation to generation. The result is that many of Azerbaijan's most treasured chefs are from Lankaran. Conveniently, Lankaran's subtropical climate is conducive to the growth of citrus fruits, grapes, rice and tea, giving talented chefs the natural ingredients with which to work. Naturally, the cuisine in Lankaran has been impacted significantly by its multicultural history, most notably from Caucasian Albania, Persia and Russia, but foods from the Talysh Khanate remain the most popular.

LAVANGI

Lankaran is the undisputed home of Lavangi. The word "Lavangi" itself roughly denotes something that is "stuffed". Broadly speaking, the thing that is usually stuffed is fish (baliq lavangi) or chicken (toyuq lavangi), and baliq lavangi is extra special in Lankaran because of the town's proximity to the sea. Traditionally, lavangi is prepared in a clay oven, though now more modern techniques are used, and an oven will work fine for the toyuq lavangi recipe I have given below.

Ingredients

2 small Cornish chickens
1 large Onion
1 cup of Walnuts
1 cup of Raisins
1 cup of Prunes
1 cup of sour Cherry-plums (or Lavashana)
50g of butter
Salt and pepper (to taste)

Method

Make sure the cavity of the chicken is clear. Rinse and pat the chicken dry, inside and out. Sprinkle the outside of the chicken generously with salt and pepper, and rub a little salt and pepper inside the cavity as well.

To make the stuffing, peel and dice the onion and fry in butter until golden brown. Blend the nuts, the raisins, prunes and cherry-plums and mix them together to create the stuffing. Add more melted butter if necessary.

Pack the stuffing into the chicken's cavity, and place your chicken on a rack set over a pan (to help the chicken roast evenly). Pour melted butter and some cherry-plum pastille over the chicken, rubbing to coat it well.

Preheat the oven to 180°C. Put both chickens in the oven and roast them for an hour until they are cooked. If the juices run clear when pierced, the chicken is ready. Allow the chicken to rest for 10 minutes before serving.

Serve either as a separate dish or together with shirin plov.

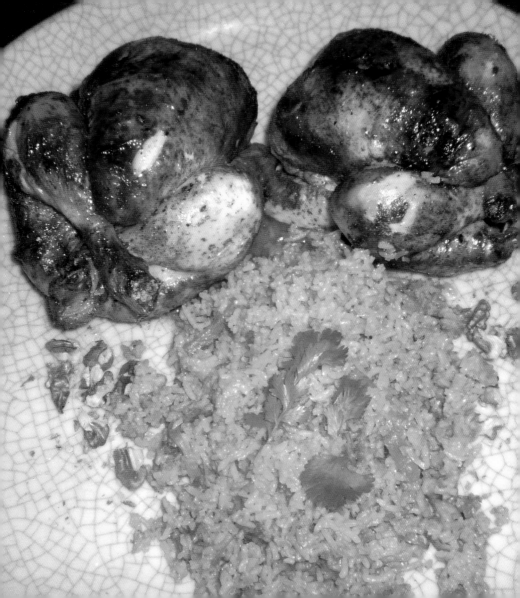

QIZIL BALIQ YOURGANDA

Qizil baliq yourganda is essentially fish in a blanket, combining fresh Caspian "salmon", which is actually a subspecies of trout, with pastry. The downside is that Salmo trutta caspiensis, the fish that is often used for this dish, is critically endangered, so look for versions with a substitute. For our home recipe, ironically enough, we will use salmon.

Ingredients
1 salmon fillet
Puff pastry dough
Olive oil
Salt and pepper (to taste)

Method
Cut salmon fillet cut into portions (roughly 6 by 15 cm) and lightly coat salmon with oil, and season with salt and pepper. Set aside.

Cut enough puff pastry dough into strips of about 2.5 cm and wrap them around the portions of salmon. Brush the top of the dough with the egg yolk. Bake in a preheated oven (at 180°C).

Before serving, drizzle with narsharab or lemon juice.

LANKARAN KULCHA

There are two types of kucha in Azerbaijan. The first, from Lankaran, is round, sweet and filled, while the second is spicier and from Sheki. Both are traditionally made in a clay oven and are eaten as snacks or with tea. Below is the recipe for the delicious Lankaran kulcha.

Ingredients
650g plain flour
10g fresh yeast
175g sugar
1 egg
25 g sour cream
Poppy seeds
150g butter
Salt
A few threads of saffron

Serves: 4-5 portions

Method
preparing the saffron infusion. Mix 450g flour, the yeast, egg, 50g butter (should be soft), 75g sugar and salt and knead well until the dough is smooth and soft. Cover with a tea-towel and leave in a warm place for 60 to 90 minutes to allow it to rise.

For the filling, blend 100g sugar and 100g butter. Add the saffron infusion and 200g flour and mix well. The filling should be crumbly.

When the dough has risen, knead it again and roll it out several times. Divide the dough into balls of around 75g and on a floured surface roll out each ball to a thickness of about 1cm.

Put a spoonful of stuffing in the centre of each, and fold the edge of the dough into the centre, pinching shut. Leave to rest for 40 minutes.

Coat the surface of the kulcha with beaten egg, sprinkle poppy seeds on top and bake in an oven preheated to 180°C for 20-25 minutes.

NARSHARAB

Though Narsharab is not a dish on its own, it is such a feature of Azerbaijani cuisine that it is impossible to omit. The Azerbaijani word **"narşərab"** comes from "nar", meaning "pomegranate", and **"şərab"**, meaning "wine". This sauce dresses meats and fish all over the caucuses, but is, in my opinion, extra special when served with the delicious fresh fish dishes of Lankaran.

Ingredients
300g pomegranate seeds
200g granulated sugar

Method
In a medium size saucepan over medium heat, cook the pomegranate seeds, sugar and 100ml water together. You are looking for the sauce to reduce and become thicker. As you start to see this happening, crush the seeds (a potato masher will do the trick).

After about 30-45 minutes the sauce should become thick. Pour the sauce through a strainer to remove seed husks.

MARY

MARY PROVINCE, TURKMENISTAN

An oasis in the vast Karakum desert, Mary lies at the heart of the cotton-growing belt and close to massive underground natural gas reserves.

Despite having exceptionally large gardens and being named the cultural capital of the Commonwealth of Independent States (an association of former Soviet republics), the city itself is not all that inspiring. However, at only 30km away it is the perfect launch-pad to go and see one of Turkmenistan's real treasures: the ancient city of Merv.

Listed as a UNESCO World Heritage Site, it is said that Merv was once the largest city in the world during the 12th century. As such, it was a political and cultural melting pot...

CHAL

Popular in the deserts of Turkmenistan and on the steppes of Kazakhstan on hot summer days, chal is fizzy, fermented camel milk. Although this may seem like an odd beverage, I am told that camel milk is actually much closer to human milk in its constitution than the milk of cows. Furthermore, fermented camel milk is reputed to have much more vitamin C than cows' milk, as well as superior antibacterial and antiviral properties.

Chal is made by allowing the camel milk to sour in a bag or jar, before adding fresh milk and allowing that too to sour. This process is repeated over the course of three or four days. Because of the way chal is prepared, and the fact that it will spoil relatively quickly, it is rather difficult to export. This means that if you want to taste this surprisingly delicious beverage, you will just have to come to Central Asia and drink it freshly made.

NARYN

NARYN PROVINCE, KYRGYZSTAN

The city of Naryn is situated on the banks of the Naryn river, which carves an eye-catching gorge that splits the city in half. Beginning life as an unspectacular fortification on the route between the Central Asian highlands and China, Naryn does not have a particularly illustrious history.

Naryn region, however, is considered the cultural heart of Kyrgyzstan, and here nomadic practices reign supreme. The highest quality shyrdaks (colourfully stitched felt rugs or wall-hangings) are made here, and can be seen in yurts across the land. Many of the centuries-old Kyrgyz culinary concoctions can be found in the valleys, grasslands or restaurants in and around Naryn's administrative capital, and include nomadic drinks and traditional dishes made from noodles and meat.

NARYN

Naryn is traditionally prepared with "aged" meat; meat that has been air-dried outside in in lower temperatures and seasoned with salt, cumin and pepper before being boiled for 2 hours. Locals will sometimes keep the meat bullion to serve as a soup with the naryn. Because of the way the meat is prepared, this is usually a winter dish. I suggest just boiling the meat beforehand to save time and effort.

Ingredients
900g boiled meat, sliced into thin ribbons (ideally a combination of lean beef and fatty lamb)

Salt, Cumin, slightly crushed
Black pepper
3 eggs
4 tbsp salt
360g all-purpose flour
240ml cottonseed oil
A meat bouillon cube

Method
Mix the eggs, flour, 1 tablespoon of salt, and 200ml of warm water to create dough and knead until smooth. Set aside for 10 minutes. Cut dough in two and flatten. Cover each with plastic wrap and set aside for 10-15 minutes.

In a large pot, boil 2 litres of water, 1 litre of meat bullion and 3 tablespoons of salt. Simmer until the dough is ready to be cooked.

Roll dough out on floured surface to roughly 2mm thickness, and cut into medium sized squares. Boil the dough by dropping in the sheet one by one. Mix so as to keep the sheets separate. Cook each for 3 minutes.

Lay the sheets out to dry before rubbing each sheet with a generous amount of cottonseed oil before stacking them. Set aside for 30 minutes. Thinly julienne the dough. Once all of the dough is cut, add a little black pepper and toss the dough. Sprinkle the meat on top of the dough and toss everything together, until ingredients are well-mixed. Jullienne raw onions, mix in black pepper and serve along with Naryn.

OROMO

Oromo is made in Naryn by rolling diced meat and onions into pasta and steaming it, and you will often see it served with sauces based on tomato puree or ayran. Incidentally, vegetarian fillings work really well in this too, but might be lucky to find such a version in Naryn, given the meat-heavy diet of the locals.

Ingredients

1 ½ cups sliced sweet potato or pumpkin
1 onion, finely chopped
450g lamb, (fat trimmed and finely diced)
Pasta dough
Salt and pepper (to taste)

Serves: 4 portions

Method

Prepare your pasta dough, set it aside to rest and prepare the filling. Finely dice the lamb, sweet potato and onion and put it all in a bowl with salt and pepper. Season the mixture with pepper and salt. Give everything a good mix.

Quarter the pasta dough and roll each quarter out as thin as you can. Place a quarter of your filling on the dough base and roll the dough into a long tube with the filling inside.

Coil the tube into a spiral. Repeat the process with the other three quarters.

Steam the coils for 45 minutes to an hour, until they are cooked through. Slice the coils into wedge shaped pieces and serve with yoghurt sauce.

CHALAP

Initially, nomads made chalap using qurut because it meant that the primary ingredient for the drink would keep for a very long time. Since then, a new version of the beverage has emerged that is made with yoghurt and carbonated in order to give it a similar longevity to its qurut-based relative.

As with maksym, zharma, and bozo, recipes vary from family to family, though it is also now being sold by two major soft drinks companies, Enesay and Shoro. Home brews can be exceptionally distinctive and should definitely be given a try if the chance presents itself, but it is fair to say that even if you like chalap, you may not like particular familial variations.

By his own admission, the founder of drinks company Shoro, Taalbyldy Egemberdiev, spent five years refining the taste of chalap (as well as maksym, zharma and bozo) for mass consumption. Even so, chalap is not everyone's cup of tea.

Interesting fact!
Mixing airan with cold water then makes chalap. It is known as a good refresher of thirst.

KUMYS

Kumys is a drink that has a special place in the heats of the Kyrgyz. Believed to contain restorative properties, kumys has been used to treat a range of diseases, including tuberculosis. Even the great Hippocrates once claimed that kumys was a drink "of longevity, joy and mental agility".

Because the shelf-life of kumys is only a few days, it is traditionally only made when the mares (female horses) are actually lactating, so industrialised kumys is usually made with cow's milk. However, to make authentic kumys, mare's milk is stored for a couple of days in a chinach (a smoke-cleaned container), after which it is mixed with fresh milk and left in the sun to ferment. It is then churned in a pishpek (a wooden tub) to create the finished article, and stored in kookors (leather bottles), ready for consumption.

Buy kumys from a Naryn roadside yurt to taste some of the best kumys in the land.

Interesting fact!
The popular Japanese soft drink Calpis models its flavor after the taste of kumis.

Osh

OSH PROVINCE, KYRGYZSTAN

Though recent times in Osh have been turbulent, particularly given the well publicised 2010 Uzbek-Kyrgyz clashes, do not let that put you off visiting this ancient city.

Osh is the oldest city in Kyrgyzstan, and genuinely one of the Silk Road's longest-standing fixtures. Estimates place the Fergana Valley town at roughly 3 millennia old, even though visible evidence of this heritage is now sparse (barring, of course, the largest outdoor market in Central Asia). There seems to be some confusion about who founded Osh, with names like Alexander the Great and King Solomon being bandied about, but there is little debate that it was levelled by the Mongols in the 13th Century, and was subsequently rebuilt before eventually being annexed by the Russian empire in the 19th Century. Furthermore, the Lenin statue that towers opposite the city administration building screams of the city's more recent Soviet past.

Despite the tragedy of the Osh riots in 2010, the mass mingling of the Kyrgyz and Uzbeks in the city has led to some delightful culinary fusions. Food in Osh draws on the fresh Fergana Valley produce, combines old world and new world ingredients, and incorporates the cooking customs of two of the great Silk Road peoples.

JARKOP

Jarkop is a dish that exemplifies the variety that is now possible in much of Central Asian cuisine with the introduction of all kinds of "New World" ingredients from Russia and beyond. Potatoes and carrots play a prominent role in this dish, and compliment the lamb that has been eaten in Kyrgyzstan from time immemorial.

Ingredients

1kg lamb (fore end or brisket)
3 onions
500g potato
300g carrot
2 tbsp tomato puree
5 cloves garlic
Dill or parsley (to taste)
100ml vegetable oil
5g each of ground red and black pepper
½ tbsp salt

Method

Cut the lam into pieces of around 10-15g, and fry in oil with high heat. Clean the carrots and dice into medium-sized cubes. Clean and slice the onions. Add the carrot and onion to the meat, as well as the tomato puree, pepper and salt before mixing well.

Cut the potatoes into large pieces, place into a saucepan and mix with the rest of the ingredients. Leave to stand on one side for about 5 minutes, then cover with water and bring to boil. Turn the temperature down to a medium heat and simmer for about 40 minutes.

Five minutes before serving, add the finely chopped garlic and decorate with green herbs to serve.

UZGEN PLOV

Is one our national dishes that pretty much every Central Asian people love.

Paloo (Kyrgyz: палоо) is the Kyrgyz version of what is generally referred to as plov in Central Asian cuisine. It consists of pieces of meat (generally mutton or beef, but sometimes chicken) fried in a large qazan (a cast-iron cauldron) and mixed with fried shredded carrots and cooked rice. The dish is garnished with whole fried garlic cloves and hot red peppers. Uzgen paloo is made with locally grown rice from the southern Uzgen District of Kyrgyzstan. Shirin paloo, a close relative of shirin plov in Azerbaijani cuisine, is a vegetarian dish in which meat is replaced with dried fruits, such as prunes, apricots, and raisins.

Paloo is the Kyrgyzified form of the Persian word polow or polo, related in etymology to pilaf. In Russian the dish is called plov (Russian: плов), in Turkic languages ash, and in Tajik osh.

CHAK-CHAK

Eaten at tea-time or as a desert, chak-chak is made from noodle dough and honey. Chak-chak is recognised as a tartar delicacy, but is now popular throughout central asia. Natural honey is a specialty in Kyrgyzstan, and this is used to produce beautiful chak-chak which can be bought in Osh's huge outdoor market.

Ingredients

300g flour
2 eggs
1-2 tbsp of sour cream or milk
Pinch of salt
2 tsp butter
340g honey
2-4 tbsp sugar.
240ml melted butter or oil.

Method

Mix eggs, sugar and butter together before salt and milk or water are added. Pour flour in and knead the stiff dough before letting it sit for 40 minutes.

Then, roll the dough out to a thin layer about 4 mm thick. Cut the dough into strips 15mm long and 4mm thick. Fry the strips in melted butter or oil until they are a golden colour, then sieve away the excess moisture.

Heat the honey together with the sugar to a syrupy consistency. Drop the strips of fried dough in this syrup chak-chak, and mix thoroughly.

Lay the Chak-chak on a slightly oiled plate and arrange it into the shape of a large thimble, and allow it to set.

JARMA

Jarma has a fascinating, but obscure history that exemplifies exactly why it is often so difficult to find just one home for various Central Asian tastes in this book.

Though nobody seems to know where jarma originally came from, it is thought that this "liquid bread" represents the very first use of barley in the nomadic context in Central Asia. Though the drink is often now be made with wheat and corn, barley jarma is what you should try if you want to day-dream yourself into the shoes of a real nomad.

Made with only organic ingredients, jarma began to be mass produced by drinks company Shoro in the mid-90s, and this makes it very easy to buy. In my experience, however, it is difficult to love. Jarma is very much the definition of "an acquired taste".

SAMARKAND

SAMARKAND PROVINCE, UZBEKISTAN

Samarkand, famed around the world for its intimate connection with the Silk Road, is every bit as impressive as you might imagine. Settled in the 5th Century BC, Samarkand is alive with the buzz of bazaars and street sellers helping it to retain the feel of an old trading hub. The city is littered with countless grand monuments to Timur that indicate the city's profound significance at the heart of Timur's old empire. Minarets poke skywards from domed mosques and ancient structures, sitting in intriguing opposition to the Soviet-style sprawl of the surrounding, modern-day business districts.

UNESCO have added the city to its World Heritage List, calling it "Samarkand – Crossroads of Cultures", and that certainly seems like an accurate description. Like Bukhara, Samarkand has brought together the traditions of peoples from across Asia, as well as acting as an intellectual and religious hub. In the kitchen, the city has made a name for itself with the famous Samarkand plov and some of Central Asia's finest wine.

SAMARKAND PLOV

Samarkand Plov is famed for being light and fluffy by the Uzbeks, made by layering meat (lamb/beef), carrot and rice before steaming it. Traditionally prepared in a Kazan.

Ingredients:
1 kg moderately fat lamb,
1 kg medium grain rice
200-250 ml vegetable frying oil
1 kg carrot
2-3 medium size onions
1-1.5 tbsp cumin
2-3 whole heads of garlic,
1-2 long hot chillies (optional)
salt to taste
5 liter heavy cast-iron cattle (kazan)

Method:
Wash the rice under the tap until clear, cover with cold water and let it soaks for a while. Cut the meat with bones into match-box pieces. Cut the carrots into 0.5x0.5 cm thick sticks. Slice onions into thin rings or half-rings. Clean heads of garlic from the remains of roots and dirt.

Heat oil in the cattle or dutch oven on a very high flame, deep-fry meat until golden-brown, in 3-4 batches. Fry the onions until golden, add meat to the cattle, stir well to prevent onion from burning. Add carrot, stir from time to time, until it starts to wilt and browns a little (15-20 min). Add 2/3 of the cumin - rub it in your palms a little to release flavor, stir gentliy to keep carrot from broking.

Lower gas to moderate, pour hot water just to cover all the goods, add salt and let it simmer for 40 min to 1.5 hours until almost all water evaporate and meat became tender and juicy. Do not stir.

Turn gas to max. Drain rice well, place it on top the meat and vegs in one layer, stick the garlic and whole chillies in it, and carefully pour boiling water over it (place a spoon or ladle on top of the rice to keep the rice layer from washaway). Cover the rice with about 2 cm of water, let it boil. Add salt to make the water a bit over-salted. When water will go down the rice, reduce the gas a bit, keeping it boils rapidly. Check when it will evaporate and absorb into rice completely - rice should remain rather al dente. Make a holes in the rice to the bottom of a vessel to check the water level.

Reduce gas to absolute min, cover tightly with the lid and let it steam 20 minutes. Turn of the heat, remove the garlic and chillies on the separate plate. Carefully mix rice with meat and carrots, if the rice tastes a bit blind add some salt, mix and let it stand for 5 minutes. Pile the plov on a big warmed plate and serve with garlic, chilies and plain thinly sliced tomato-sweet onions-chili-salt salad.

MASTAVA

A dish best served hot in the cold winters, mastava is a meat and rice shurpa (soup). Its unique taste comes from the meat being sautéed (a fairly unusual practice with Central Asian shurpas), and, much like soup in the west, it is often served to cure fevers and high temperatures.

Ingredients
1 tbsp olive oil
230g lamb, cubed
½ onion, sliced
1 carrot, sliced
1 turnip, sliced
80g tomato paste
3 cups chicken broth
¼ tsp salt
70g rice
¼ cup cilantro
2 tbsp sour cream
¼ tsp pepper

Method
Heat some olive oil in a good-sized pot over medium heat. Sauté the lamb until it is lightly browned (about 5 minutes), but make sure you do not overcook; it is important that the meat remains moist.

Add the chopped onion, carrot, and turnip and sauté for another 5 minutes. Add the tomato paste and chicken broth. Bring the mixture to a boil. Add salt, pepper and rice. Reduce heat and simmer for 20 minutes. Add cilantro and a dollop of our sour cream before serving.

WINE

As the Russian Empire tore through Central Asia, the region was flooded with traders ready to take advantage of any natural resources that were to be discovered there. On discovering an incredibly sweet grape known locally as "Taifi", Dmitriy Filatov, a Russian merchant, founded a winery in 1868. Within 4 years Filatov was winning awards in Paris and Antwerp for the quality of the wine he managed to produce.

In 1927, the winery's fame would explode with the arrival of Russian wine-maker, Michaer Khorvrenko, who increased the efficiency of production of famed wines such as Gulyakandoz, Shirin, Aleatiko, and Kabernet likernoe (Cabernet dessert wine). Today, Khovrenko Winery in Samarkand is the oldest and most famous winery in Uzbekistan. There is a fascinating museum attached to the winery if you would like to learn more, and now they produce wines from a vast array of different kinds of grapes, as well as a number of other beverages.

SHEKI
SHEKI REGION, AZERBAIJAN

Tumbling down the slopes of the Greater Caucuses mountain range is the historic town of Sheki. Sheki is apparently named after the Sakas people, who stumbled upon the territory having journeyed from modern-day Iran. Settlements around Sheki date back to roughly 2700 years ago, and the city would later operate as a major hub for the ancient Albanians, before changing hands between rulers of many empires including the Georgian Kingdom and the Mongol Empire.

Since many historical artefacts from Sheki's time as part of the Sheki Khanate (existing in the 18th and 19th Century) have been well preserved, the town is a tourist hotbed and offers sights such as the nail-less Palace of Sheki Khans and Sheki Castle. A great deal of Azerbaijani culture has been packed into this small town. Take particular note of its unique architecture, spoken dialect, art and deserts. Looking out over Sheki's famed red-rooftops, indulge your sweet tooth by trying Sheki's renowned Sheki Pakhlava

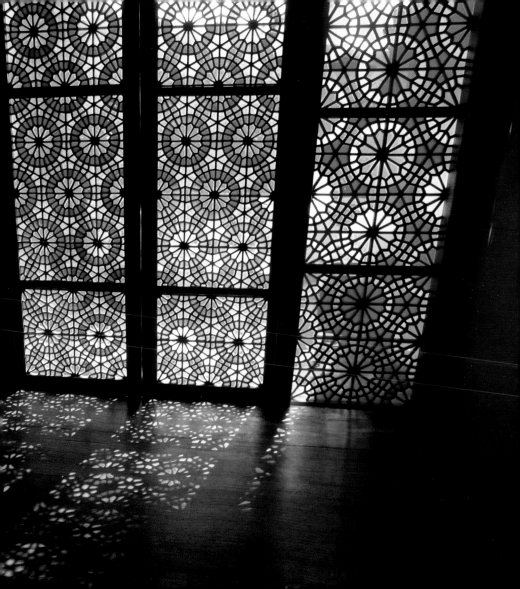

SHEKI GYURZA

Gyurza is an Azerbaijani dumpling soup cooked in a lamb broth. The master chefs of Sheki have made the dish their own by artistically braiding the edges of the dumplings together using a special technique. You can get gyurza all over the country, but nowhere will it look like this.

Ingredients

450g lamb (for broth)
2 onions
1/2 tsp saffron or turmeric
Salt
350g flour
1 egg
250g grounded lamb or beef (for filling)
Pepper (to taste)

Method

Boil the meat in a covered saucepan. Add chopped onion, a pinch of saffron or turmeric, and season with salt to taste. Simmer for about an hour. Strain through a fine mesh colander and set aside. Keep the broth.

Make dough by kneading flour, egg, a pinch of salt and a little water together until it is soft and elastic. Shape the dough into a ball, cover with cling-film, and set aside for 20 minutes.

In a bowl, combine the grounded meat with finely chopped onion, and season with salt and pepper. Mix the filling well and set aside.

Roll out the dough on a floured surface into a large thin circle (1-2 mm thick). Cut the dough into circles and place a teaspoon of filling into the middle of each circle. Fold them into half-moon shapes and pinch the edges together leaving a small opening in each. Put the dumplings in the boiling broth and gently stir. Simmer until dough is tender (10 mins).

Serve broth and dumplings together and sprinkle with dried mint or fresh chopped cilantro. Serve hot with vinegar and chopped garlic mix.

PITI

Cooked in a clay oven and eaten from a deep dish known as a "kyasa", variations of piti span from the Mediterranean to the Caucuses. The dish gets its name from the Turkic word "bitdi" which means "end of festivity" because it is said that the dish is so nutritious that anyone who finishes a portion will be too full to want anything else.

Ingredients

1kg mutton or veal (brisket or shoulder)
1 onion
200g chick peas
150g chestnuts
8-10 prunes
3 pinches turmeric
Salt, pepper and sumac (to taste)

Serves: 4 portions

Method

Cut the meat into medium-sized chunks. Put the whole peeled onion into a saucepan (do not cut off the stem) and add the chick peas and chestnuts with 950ml water. Boil on high heat and skim residue from the broth when necessary. Reduce heat and cover, allowing the mixture to simmer for 2-3 hours. Add prunes and turmeric 30 minutes before the ingredients are ready.

Add salt, pepper and sumac to taste. Sprinkle salt, pepper and sumac in a bowl, layer with chunks of bread and pour over the remaining broth to create a soup to accompany the main dish.

DOVGA

It is the freshness of the ingredients around Sheki that make this dish a hit with the locals. Cooks combine yoghurt, herbs, rice and chickpeas (and sometimes even meat) to create the unique flavour of dogva. Expect to see it served hot in the winter, and refreshingly cool in the summer.

Ingredients

2l thick plain yoghurt
75g chickpeas
1 egg
50g plain flour
50g short grain rice (the more rice, the thicker the dovga)
Large bunches of coriander, dill and mint (necessary)
Mountain parsley, chervil, spinach leaves or beet tops, celery tops and young wild leeks (if available)

Serves: 7-8 portions

Method

Put the chickpeas in a pan of water, bring to a boil and simmer for 30 minutes. Don't overcook (they will cook further in the dovga). Wash and finely dice the herbs.

Put 200ml of yoghurt into a bowl, add the egg and mix well. Add the flour and rice and mix until the flour has been absorbed.

Put the mixture and the rest of the yoghurt in a large saucepan. Gradually add 1 litre of water and stir well. Place over a medium heat and bring to a boil, stirring all the time.

When the dovga has begun to boil, add the chopped herbs. Lower the heat and simmer until the rice is cooked (about 10-15 minutes), stirring frequently.

When serving (and not before), you can add salt to taste. Serve dovga warm or cold according to your preference.

GIRMABADAM

One of the sweets for which Sheki is famed, Girmabadam is made using nuts and coriander seeds. Girmabadam is exceptionally sweet and very moreish, so try not to get hooked!

Ingredients

675g granulated sugar
275g shelled almonds or hazelnuts
2 egg whites
75g rice flour
A drop of citric acid
Pinch of coriander seeds

Serves: 8-10 portions

Method

Make syrup by mixing the sugar, 500ml water and citric acid in a saucepan and slowly bringing to a boil. Allow to simmer until most of the moisture has evaporated and caramel is left. Beat the caramel and allow it to cool slightly (50/60°C), before adding the egg whites and beating the mixture until it has turned white. Add the crushed hazelnuts and coriander seeds and mix well.

Shape the girmabadam into rectangles roughly 15 by 8cm and half a centimetre thick. When cool, the mixture should be brittle. Sprinkle browned rice flour over the top of the girmabadam and serve.

SHEKI PAKHLAVA

Sheki Pakhlava is traditionally made in a huge, round pan approximately a metre in diameter. The batter is cooked in delicately criss-crossed flat webs (irishta), before being carefully laid on top of each other. Creating these layers is very difficult indeed, and it is a skill that has been honed by chefs in Sheki over generations. Do not feel bad if you fail a few times!

Ingredients

450g high quality Basmati rice powder (or make your own)
450g nuts
600g cups granulated sugar
3 tbsp honey
½ tsp ground cardamom
½ tsp ground coriander
2 tbsp lemon juice
2 tbsp saffron infusion

Method

Gradually mix water into the rice powder until you achieve a consistency like pancake batter.

Pre-heat a large frying pan over medium heat and grease it with melted butter. Fill a pastry bag with the batter and cut off the tip. Quickly, and without stopping, criss-cross thin strips of batter in the pan.

Once the irishta is ready, carefully remove it from the pan and set aside. You should be able to make about 14 (useable) layers. Stack them on top of each other.

Blend the nuts, mix them with the ground cardamom and coriander and prepare the saffron infusion (see shirin plov – p??). Set aside.

Mix sugar with 350ml cups of water in a saucepan and boil together. Add honey and lemon juice, and stir. Remove from heat when mixed.

Remove the top 6 layers of the irishta stack, cover the bottom 8 layers with filling and replace the top 6. Coat the top with the saffron infusion.

Fry the pakhlava in butter over low heat, until the bottom of pakhlava becomes golden. Pour half of the hot syrup all over the pakhlava. Set aside for an hour. Heat the remaining syrup and pour it on. Cover and set aside for 12 hours. Cut into squares.

AYRAN

Ayran is a drink that is popular throughout the Turkic world. While incredibly simple to make, all kinds of flavours can be added to make the ayran your own. Almost everyone I have asked advocates the health benefits of ayran, and insist that nothing goes better with spicy meat dishes.

Ingredients
300g plain yogurt
1 tsp salt

Serves: 4 portions

Method
Put 300ml water, the yoghurt and the salt in a blender and mix for about 35-40 seconds before pouring into glasses. You should see froth at the top of the drink, and ideally it should not be too thick.

TASHKENT

TASHKENT PROVINCE, UZBEKISTAN

With a multi-ethnic population of close to three million people, Tashkent lays a strong claim to being Central Asia's premier city. Initially subjected to strong Turkic and Sogdian influence, Tashkent became Muslim in the 8th Century. As with so many cities in this region, it was levelled in the 13th Century by the Mongols and eventually came under Russian rule in 1865.

Though the Uzbek capital lacks instant appeal, give it a little time and you might find yourself falling for its eccentricity. Tashkent is a city that contains the sublime and the idiosyncratic, with an array of medieval buildings and spacious parks sitting on gridded Soviet avenues alongside glitzy skyscrapers and fantastic bazaars.

Unsurprisingly, this is a city that provides all manner of quality international foods. However, Tashkent has not forgotten its culinary roots. If you visit the Old City, chaykhanas (tea-houses) and small family-run restaurants are abundant and filled with colourfully-dressed women and men trying not to drop shashlik on their chapans (quilted coats). The huge plov centre, "Osh Markazi", is also definitely worth a visit.

DYMLAMA

Dymdama is a classic Uzbek harvest stew, incorporating all manner of fresh produce. Though the recipe is altered slightly by each family, tomatoes, peppers, potatoes and carrots are mainstays, and the dish is usually made in the spring or summer when vegetables are at their most plentiful.

Ingredients
500g fat
1kg mutton
1kg tomatoes
500g carrots
1kg cabbage
1kg potatoes
500g onions
2-3 cloves garlic
300g green pepper
Spicy greens, red and black pepper, salt (to taste)

Method
Cut the fat into large chunks, slice the mutton and the carrots, chop the cabbage and onion, and quarter the tomatoes.

Put the fat and the meat in a large pot. Sprinkle the meat with onion and garlic, before putting in the potatoes, carrots, cabbage and whole pods of green pepper. Add chopped herbs, pepper, and salt to taste and bring to a boil. Reduce the heat and allow to simmer for 60 to 90 minutes. Sprinkle the dymdama with greens and pepper to serve.

CHUCHVARA

Chuchvara are small Uzbek dumplings that are somewhat similar to tortellini. Because of Islamic dietary requirements, chuchvara are made without pork, and throughout Tashkent you may see chuchvara served with soup, vinegar sauce or sour cream.

Ingredients
240g all-purpose flour
1 egg
1 tsp salt
230g minced/ground beef (ideally lean)
1 large onion
1/2 tsp ground cumin
1/2 tsp ground black pepper
Salt (to taste)

Serves: 4 portions

Method
Mix together the salt and flour before adding 180ml warm water and the egg to make the dough. Knead the dough for 5-6 minutes and cover with cling film or a bowl. Let it sit for 10 to 20 minutes.

Dice the onion and mix with the beef and spices, before putting aside. Roll the dough out to a thickness of 1-2mm, using flour to prevent the dough from sticking.

Fold the dough in half and make 2 inch-wide cuts to make separate ribbons. Make sure that the dough isn't sticky by sprinkling flour between the layers as necessary. Place a small amount of the beef, onion and spice mix inside each ribbon and pinch the edges together to seal them.

Boil the chuchvara in water (approx. 950ml) and add ½ tbsp salt. Once they have risen to the surface, stir gently and simmer for 15 minutes before serving.

LAPSHA

Traditionally lapsha, literally meaning "noodles", was made by hand and used as a base for soups that were eaten at funerals. Eventually, the dish evolved and became so popular that it is now consumed everywhere and anywhere. Various combinations of beef, fish and vegetables make the range of lapsha soups quite substantial.

Ingredients
100ml melted butter
1 1/2 teaspoons salt
6 large eggs
600g all-purpose flour

Method
Bring 100ml water to a boil in a large saucepan. Dissolve the butter in the boiling water and whisk well. Allow to cool.

In a large mixing bowl, whisk together the salt and eggs, while gradually adding the water and butter mixture. Add 600ml flour, 100ml at a time, and mix well.

When dough is ready, place it on a lightly floured surface and knead for about 10 minutes. Cut the dough into pieces to form dough balls the size of an orange. Roll out each dough ball as thin as possible.

Preheat the oven to 150°C and place dough circles on a large round pizza cooking sheet. Dry each dough circle in the preheated oven (20 minutes) but do not brown. Cut each piece of dough into very thin strands, spread slices on cookie sheets and heat in a preheated 175°C until crisp (20 minutes), moving the strands at least twice during process.

Cool completely and store in noodles glass jars with a tight fitting lid. Serve with soups.

ACHICHUK SALAD

Achichuk salad is a very simple dish but an integral part of Uzbekistan's culinary landscape. The salad is usually served as a side, goes really well with the heavier meat dishes, and is exceptionally refreshing when made with fresh tomatoes and eaten on hot summer afternoons.

Ingredients
1 tomato
1 chili pepper
½ large onion
Coriander and basil
Salt (to taste)

Serves: 1 portion

Method
Cut onion into thin strips and soak in cold water for 15-20 minutes. Drain the water and squeeze the onion gently to stimulate the flavour. Cut the tomatoes into thin slices. Clean the chili peppers and cut them into thin slices. Chop the coriander and crush the basil. Arrange the ingredients and add a little salt.

MILK RICE BOTKO

Ingredients
700g ground rice
150g golden gram, pre-soaked
4l milk
150g butter
100g pumpkin, sliced
Salt (to taste)
Fruits and berries (optional)

Method
Bring the milk to a boil. Wash and sift the ground rice and pour into the boiling milk. Add the pre-soaked golden gram with a pinch of salt, cover and cook on low heat. Stir the botko regularly to prevent it from burning.

When the rice begins to swell, add the sliced pumpkin. Once ready, allow the botko to cool slightly. Serve in bowls and top with a little melted butter. Toss in some fruits and berries to add some extra flavour if you wish.

TURKISTAN

SOUTH KAZAKHSTAN PROVINCE, KAZAKHSTAN

Turkistan is a special place. Baking in the intense summer heat in the Syr-Darya Valley, Turkistan stands as ancient testament to the architectural prowess of Timur and his people. The highlight of the town is the 600-year-old domed mazar (grave building) built atop the grave of Kozha Akhmed Yasaui, the famous Sufi sheik and mystical poet who lived in the town in the 12ᵗʰ Century.

Yasaui is considered to be the first great Muslim holy man from the Turkic peoples, and is highly revered for bringing the word of God to Central Asian steppe through the use of beautifully constructed Turkic poems and sermons. Such was Yasaui's influence among the people in the region, locals have come to believe that three pilgrimages to Turkestan equate to one hajj to Mecca (though this is widely disputed in the Muslim community).

A portrait of manmade beauty framed by the desert, Turkistan is a place where customs, like its architecture, have been preserved.

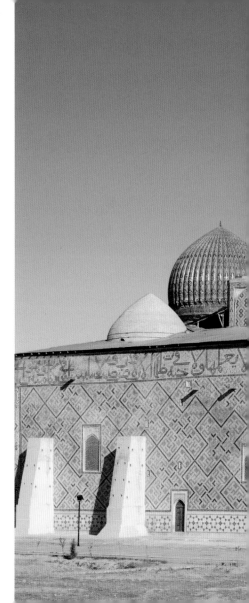

KAZY

Kazy could be roughly described as a horse-meat sausage that originated from Turkic groups in Central Asia. It is now immensely popular in Kazakhstan, and has secured its place on the Kazakh dastarkhan (eating place).

The fact that horse fat does not easily freeze means that kazy was easy for travellers to eat quickly on the move. Moreover, eating kazy initially represented wealth. Only the rich could afford to butcher horses for food as these horses required special treatment. I have been informed that these horses often grew so fat that zhigits (expert horsemen) had to be hired to wrap their stomachs and carefully bring them down from their mountain pastures so as not to rupture their intestine walls.

Traditionally, flesh from around the ribs of the horse is dried for 5 to 7 hours, allowing the blood to drain, before being seasoned and stuffed into the cleaned intestine. After the ends of these long sausages have been tied, they are left to dry in the sun for a week, or smoked for 12 to 18 hours, before being boiled and served in slices with onion and seasonal vegetables.

TURKMENBASHI

BALKAN PROVINCE, TURKMENISTAN

In 1717, Russian troops docked their boats and established a settlement where the dry Oxus riverbed met the Caspian Sea. Led by Prince Alexander Bekovich, their plan was to use the riverbed to march across the desert to the north and take Khiva. They named their settlement Krasnovodsk, and though they failed spectacularly in their quest, the name stuck until 1993 when the then president, Saparmurat Niyazov, gave the city his self-proclaimed title "Turkmenbashi" ("Leader of the Turkmen").

After the creation of the Trans-Caspian railway, Krasnovodsk began to expand. The mid-1900s brought thousands of Japanese prisoners-of-war, sent to build roads and develop buildings for this budding Caspian base. With some charming beaches, an adequate supply of cafes and restaurants and a profitable oil industry, Turkmenbashi's demographics are dominated by Russians, Turkmen and Azerbaijanis, though there is also a sprinkling of western oil workers.

The city's predominantly Russian past is evident in its restaurants, with dishes like Golubsti and Pelmeni getting a foothold.

BELUGA STURGEON CAVIAR

The Beluga Sturgeon is a gigantic, late-maturing fish that swims exclusively in the waters of the Caspian Sea, and can live to be over 100 years old. These animals often take 20 years to reach maturity and have been known to grow to 1000kg. The roe (or eggs) of these immense fish is harvested by the nations that boarder the Caspian Sea in order to produce Caviar.

The eggs that are used for caviar often vary in colour from black to light grey, with the lighter eggs being harvested from the older fish, making them more valuable. These eggs will regularly fetch thousands of dollars per kilo, but that is nothing compared to "Almas". Produced only in the relatively pollution-free south of the Caspian, Almas is caviar made from the eggs of a rare albino beluga sturgeon approaching 100 years old, and is the world's most expensive food. Should you want to try it, this "black gold" will set you back upwards of $34,000 per kilo. Such is the quality of these high-grade caviars that they are usually eaten by themselves on toast, though some extras may be served as palette-cleansers. Because of the caviar trade, Beluga Sturgeon are now considered critically endangered, so be aware that what you see for sale may well have been irresponsibly sourced.

GOLUBSTI

Golubsti is a Russian stuffed cabbage dish brought to Turkmenbashi by the Russians who settled here. Golubsti is often made using rice or buckwheat groats, but for our recipe I have used millet. This is a dish that works with a range of ingredients, so don't be afraid to experiment.

Ingredients

1 whole head cabbage
200g millet, rinsed and drained, (reserve cooking liquid)
50g salted pork, chopped
2 large carrots, finely chopped
1 large onion, finely chopped
2 large eggs
Salt and pepper (to taste)
Hot peppers (optional)
2 tbsp butter
2 tbsp all-purpose flour
4 tbsp tomato paste
8 tbsp sour cream

Serves: 18 portions (small)

Preparation

Pre-heat the oven to 325°C and remove the core from the cabbage. Boil whole head in a large pot, covered, in salted water until soft enough to pull off 18 individual leaves.

Cut out the thick stem from each leaf, leaving the leaf intact. Chop the remaining cabbage and place it in the bottom of a large, deep cooking dish.

In a large frying pan, sauté the chopped salt pork, carrots and onions until tender, and allow to cool. Place the millet in a saucepan, and cover with 2 cups broth or salted water. Bring to a boil, before draining but keep the broth. Mix the parboiled millet with salt pork-carrot-onion mixture. Mix in eggs, salt and pepper and hot pepper.

Place about 1/2 cup of millet filling on each cabbage leaf. Roll away from you to encase the filling. Roll filling into the cabbage leaf and put in your deep dish.

In a small saucepan, make a roux with the butter and flour, cooking until golden. Whisk in the tomato paste and sour cream, adding a few tablespoons of broth if necessary, to get a smooth consistency. Add 1 cup broth and bring to a boil. Pour sour cream-tomato paste sauce on top of cabbage rolls. Cover and place in oven. Cook until cabbage and millet are tender (1 hour).

PELMENI

Filled with anything from pork to sauerkraut depending on the preferences of the chef, pelmeni are Russian mini-dumplings that are often served with red-wine vinegar, black pepper and melted butter. These dumplings get their name because of their shape, with "pelmeni" describing their ear-like appearance.

Ingredients
2 large eggs
1 tbsp vegetable oil
1 tsp salt
420g all-purpose flour
1 large onion, finely grated
230g ground pork
230g ground beef
1½ tsp salt
½ tsp pepper

Serves: 80 to 100 portions (mini-dumplings)

Method

Mix the eggs, 150ml water, oil, salt and half the flour and knead. Add the remaining flour as you knead until the dough on a floured surface until it is soft. Wrap in cling-film and set aside for 30 minutes.

In a bowl, mix onion, meat, salt and pepper until thoroughly mixed.

Cut dough into 8 equal pieces and roll each into a finger-width cylinder. Cut each one into 10 pieces. Roll each of the 10 pieces into a 5cm diameter circle. Spread 1 teaspoon of filling on the circle, leaving space at the edges. Pinch the edges together to make a half-moon, ensuring that there is no trapped air. Place on a baking sheet.

Boil a large saucepan of salted water, and drop in 10 pelmeni at a time. When they rise to the surface, boil for an 1-2 more minutes, and remove from the water. Repeat with the process with the remaining pelmeni. Serve with melted butter, red-wine vinegar, black pepper, and sour cream, if desired.

MASHKHURDA

Meat, Mung Bean And Rice Soup

Ingredients

2 tbsp olive oil
450g beef or lamb, cubed
1 Medium Onion, chopped
1 Medium Carrot, chopped
80g mung beans
1.2l beef broth
1 can tomato paste
50g cup rice
1 medium potato, chopped
Salt and Pepper (to taste)
1 bunch scallions, chopped
Yogurt (optional)

Serves: 4

Method

Sauté the meat in oil until well browned. Add onion and carrot, and fry for 10 minutes. Add the broth and beans, and simmer for 40 minutes.

Add tomato paste, rice and potato and simmer for 15 minutes. Add salt and pepper and allow to simmer for 5 more minutes.

To serve, ladle the soup into bowls and sprinkle with scallions and dollop of yogurt if you wish.

BUGLAMA KOVOQ

Steamed pumpkin – appetiser

Ingredients
500g pumpkin
20g butter
20g sugar

Method

Remove all seeds from the pumpkin and chop it into small cubes. Coat each of these cubes with melted butter and then dust with sugar. Steam the pumpkin cubes for 30 minutes. You can serve the buglama kovoq hot or cold depending on your preference.

YAKHNA TIL

Boiled tongue – appetiser

Ingredients
1kg beef tongue
2 carrots
2 onions
1 head of garlic
1 bay leaf, dill and salt (to taste)

Method
Chop up the carrots and onions and dice the garlic and seasonings. Scrub the tongue well, and put in a pot of cold water (about 1.5l), and simmer gently. Add chopped carrots, onions, garlic, and seasonings.

When done, remove from broth and place tongue in cold water in order to skin it more easily. Cut skinned tongue diagonally into very thin slices. Serve before the tongue has cooled completely and garnish with greens.

Though not necessary, you can flesh out the salad with o pad the salad out with cucumbers, tomatoes, lettuce, and other fresh and pickled vegetables.

FRIED PASTIES FILLED WITH MEAT

Dough
1 package active dry yeast
¼ teaspoon sugar
3 cups all-purpose flour
1 cup lukewarm milk (110°F to 115°F)

Filling
1½ pounds beef, finely ground
¾ cup finely chopped onions
1 teaspoon salt
¼ teaspoon freshly ground black pepper
3 to 4 tablespoons butter
2 to 3 tablespoons vegetable oil

Method

Combine the meat, onions, salt and pepper in a large bowl and knead with your hands or beat with a large spoon until smooth. On a lightly floured surface roll the dough into a circle about ½ inch thick, then cut out 16 circles with a 4½-inch cookie cutter.

Place 5 teaspoons of filling on each circle and moisten the edges of the dough with cold water. Fold up all the edges of the dough, enclosing the filling and making a flat, round cake.

Preheat the oven to 250°F. In a 10- to 12-inch heavy skillet set over high heat, melt 3 tablespoons of butter in 2 tablespoons of oil. When the fat begins to turn light brown, add half of the flat cakes and cover the pan.

Reduce the heat to moderate and cook for about 10 minutes on each side, or until the cakes are crisp and brown. Then transfer them to an ovenproof platter and keep warm in the low oven while you cook the remaining cakes.

Add additional butter and oil to the pan if necessary. Serve at once.

TOUR PROGRAM "CULINARY TOUR" IN KYRGYZSTAN

Culinary Tour with Ak Sai Travel

Highlights:
- Taste 7 cuisines made by 7 families of 7 nations
- Burana historical complex (UNESCO site) on the Great Silk Road
- Easy walks in Tien Shan mountains
- Nomadic Traditions of Kyrgyz Republic

Ak-Sai Travel Culinary Tour combines the best of Kyrgyzstan cuisine, culture and food with unique historic sights of the Great Silk Road. The Culinary Tour includes visiting several different families with various ethnic background, traditions and cooking ritual. All this helps to combine elements of a historical tour with a culinary adventure! On the trip you will not only have an opportunity to sample some of the finest food offerings from various nations, but also meet the locals.

Program:
Day 1 **(Korean Cuisine)**: Airport – Bishkek city.
Day 2 **(Uzbek Cuisine)**: Full day sightseeing Bishkek city.
Day 3 **(Kyrgyz Cuisine)**: Bishkek city – Chon Kemin valley.
Day 4 **(Russian Cuisine)**: Chon Kemin valley – Cholpon Ata town at Issyk Kul Lake, Northern shore.
Day 5 **(Dungan Cuisine)**: Cholpon Ata town – Karakol town.
Day 6 **(Uighur Cuisine)**: Karakol town – Kochkor village.
Day 7 **(Kazakh Cuisine)**: Kochkor village – Bishkek city.
Day 8: Bishkek city - airport.

Bishkek, Kyrghyz Republic
Phone: 996 /312/ 90 16 16
E-mail: info@ak-sai.com, office@ak-sai.com
Web: ak-sai.com, mice.kg

AK-SAI TRAVEL
www.ak-sai.com

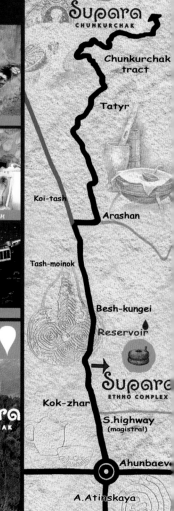

Hotel
ALPINIST
Kyrgyzstan   Bishkek

113 Panfilov Street, Bishkek, Kyrgyzstan
Tel.: +996-312-699 621   Fax: +996-312-595 647
E-mail:alpinist@elcat.kg   www.alpinist.centralasia.kg

HOTEL

ShahPalace
BISHKEK

www.shahpalace.kg   +996(312) 986822

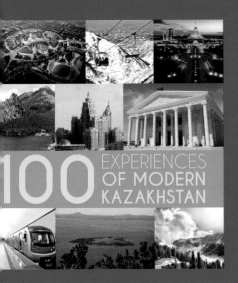

100 EXPERIENCES OF MODERN KAZAKHSTAN

The modern Kazakhstan is a country with a rapidly growing economy, a stable political system and a unique culture. During its 550 years of established statehood history, the country has played a key role in implementing the main geopolitical mission - assistance in integration and formation of a common space of peace and creativeness in the Great Steppe. Over the years of independence, Kazakhstan has seen unparalleled progress, having become an example of stable growth and stability. Today, Kazakhstan has taken a centre stage as a dynamic leader in the Eurasian region. The country is a home for over 100 various ethnic groups, it contributes to expansion of inter-religious dialogue, as well as playing a key role in ensuring regional and global security.

Kazakhstan is a real must visit place with wonderful places. It boasts emerald green pine forests and miles of big canyons. The mountains host a variety of adventures in every season from skiing, snowboarding, and skating to hiking, riding and camping. Apart from varied and stunning natural beauty, the country also boasts its vibrant cities and rich traditions.

ISBN: 978-1-910886-15-1
AVAILABLE ON AMAZON.COM

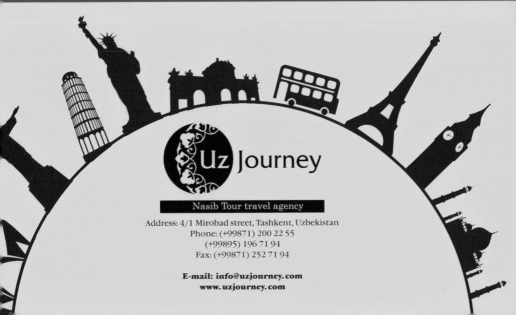